Derren Brown U

Theories, Methods and

Secrets.

Copyright 2017 Steve Piers.

Notes

Introduction

Magical Thinking

Finding the Method

Bringing it all Together

The Methods Revealed in this Book

The Content and Format of this Book

Preshow Work and Dual Reality

Watching the Performances

Something Wicked This Way Comes – Explanation

An Evening of Wonders – Explanation

Enigma – Explanation

Svengali – Explanation

Infamous – Explanation

Miracle – Explanation

Underground / Secret - Explanation

Afterword – The Masked Magician

<u>Notes</u>

Introduction

I will never forget the end of Derren Brown's Enigma show at the Liverpool Empire Theatre. After three standing ovations (the last of which was over ten minutes long), the 2,300 strong audience spilled out of the building, with most of them excitedly discussing what they had just seen. I heard them coming up with their own theories and methods. As a magician, I understood some of the magic principles on display and I was surprised at the complexity of the ideas that the general public had come up with. Working as a magician makes it difficult for me to watch a performance through the eyes of a non-magician, and it was fascinating to me to hear theories that used actual mind reading skills and psychic abilities, rather than simple magical principles.

Let's say a magician offers you a choice from a deck of cards, and then reads your mind to determine which one you picked. The mind reading element of the trick should be the focus of the audience's attention. The magician should spend the overwhelming majority of the routine demonstrating their psychic abilities to the audience. This approach draws all attention away from the fact that the performer is a magician and has simply forced a specific card, whilst creating the illusion of a free choice. The trick becomes a demonstration of mind reading, of psychic powers and the style of presentation is completely different to the magical performers you've seen in the past. There's not a glamorous assistant in sight, no flashy magical cabinets, no tigers or doves, and yet you're still watching a magician performing magic, it's just presented as something different. Something much better.

Watching Enigma, I became fascinated by the logistics of performing a magic show to such a massive audience. Imagine the pressure on the performer. When tricks go wrong, as they sometimes do, how do you ad-lib and move on with an audience of that size?

When I perform my current magic act, it lasts just over an hour and it was rehearsed meticulously over a period of six months. Trapdoors got stuck, elastic bands broke, audience volunteers forgot the card they chose, and so on. It's impossible to predict every single eventuality that can cause a problem with the routine and some of my more complex methods had to be dropped to remove the risk of anything going wrong. When a trick fails midway through, the magician can try to cover it up with 'multiple-outs' where the intended effect is dropped and the magician works with what they have to salvage the routine and bring it to an ending without revealing the failure. How much easier it would be to perform a routine that simply cannot go wrong. With the reassurance that the mechanics of the trick are straightforward enough to guarantee success, the next stage in the design of the show is to dress up the simple effect and make it appear more complex.

An Example.

Here's a trick that's designed to be so simple that it cannot fail. I'll explain the process, then we'll dress up the performance to make the simple trick a million times bigger and better.

This trick uses 'multiple outs' in its conclusion and this makes it completely safe – there's no possibility that the trick can go wrong. It's also an effect that I make and sell in my magic shop. The magician removes three large playing cards from an envelope, and places them face up on the table. He hands a magic wand to the spectator who is asked to wave the wand over the three cards. Whenever they feel ready they should tap just one card with the wand. The spectator then turns over the card they chose. Printed on the back it says "you will choose this card".

On sale in my shop for only five pounds, this trick comes with a disclaimer – if you buy it, please try to remember how you felt during the performance. Keep in mind that you were fooled. I explain this because many people buy the trick after a demonstration, just because they want to know how it works. But if I ask them how *they* think it works they sound like the Derren Brown theatre audience that night in Liverpool. The theories can be extremely complicated and often rely on chance, coincidence, luck, probability and sleight of hand. Like many magic tricks the explanation is simple, so simple in fact that it can be disappointing. The audience know that the card they turned over has "you will choose this card" printed on the back. Usually, the first thing they do is to turn over the two remaining cards and check there is nothing printed on each of them. There isn't of course (that would be too easy!) but the spectator never asks to look inside the envelope that the performer is still holding in their hands. This irrelevant detail is the key to the method. Inside the envelope is a piece of white card, printed with the message "You will choose the King of Clubs". The other seemingly irrelevant item in this trick is the wand. Why did the magician give a wand to the performer? Surely they could have just as easily pointed to the card they wanted to choose? Again, the spectator never looks too closely at the wand. If they did, they would see it has a message printed along the length, "You will pick the Two of Diamonds".

That's what we call a multiple out – three different endings to the trick. The spectator hasn't seen the trick before, so they make the assumption that I would have asked them to turn over the card, whichever they chose. That's not how it works. If they choose the King of Clubs,

I'll continue the trick by asking them to look inside the envelope that I have been holding the whole time. If they choose the Two of Diamonds, I'll ask them to look at the wand they are holding. The spectator never queries the wand or the envelope if the outcome of the trick results in them turning over the card on the table. Likewise, if they are told to look at the wand, they are too busy being baffled by the message on the wand to start questioning why I have been holding the envelope all the way through the trick. It never fails. Every option is covered.

This is a perfect trick in my opinion. For a start, I've been performing this for years in my shop and the only people who have ever called me on it were people who have studied magic. No ordinary member of the public (I really don't like the term 'laypeople') has *ever* worked it out and I have sold many sets over the years as many people pay up just to find the method. They can initially seem disappointed in the simplicity of the secret, but then of course they take their new trick home, and bamboozle their friends with it.

I wanted to explain this trick at the beginning of my book, because it sets the tone for what's to follow.

Showmanship.

It's important that in demonstrating this trick I create a performance. It's easy to say "Choose a card", then "OK, look at the wand" and the trick would last about thirty seconds. In this way the trick is presented as nothing more than a fun little puzzle to be solved, but it's not magic. We need to make this trick bigger through the presentation. I'll do this by talking to the spectator and setting the scene whilst I lay out the cards on the table. I'll shift the focus away from the cards themselves and instead I will tell the spectator that I want to perform an experiment that will teach them about the way in which our free choices can be manipulated by suggestion and clever use of language. We're going to learn something about how the brain works.

"It's puzzling, but it means that you can convince people that you know things about themselves, predict ways people will behave, even to the point where you can make people do what you want them to do. I'll show you something really simple. I've got three playing cards here, and I want you to choose one of them. Don't choose it yet, because I want you to really think about it. You can see we have two picture cards and one number card. Perhaps you think I want you to choose the number card because the other two are more elaborate so it stands out as different. Or maybe, that's a ruse to make you ignore the number card, and I want you to concentrate on one of the two remaining picture cards. Now, I can see from the way you are holding your handbag that you are right handed, so If I wanted you to pick a specific card perhaps I

would lay that out on the right? The important point here is I really want you to think about your choice. I want you to know it's a completely free choice."

After the card has been selected, we take a moment to ask why they chose that card, because the reveal of the prediction message signifies the end of the trick. The choice has now been made and this offers me a moment of down-time as the spectator's job is done and they can relax. I can take this opportunity to casually take back the wand or put down the envelope, depending on which card was chosen. This whole approach makes the performance more than simple coincidence or trickery; it becomes a demonstration of psychology and mind control.

Derren Brown is, in my opinion the best at creating this kind of bigger effect from a small method. Derren and his team create unbelievable miracles, and the showmanship makes even the smallest effect something extremely special and memorable. A simple magical principal allows the performer to focus on the showmanship and presentation.

Nothing can be allowed to go wrong.

Our example trick is perfect – nothing can be allowed to go wrong in a performance and nothing can go wrong with this trick as every option is covered. The worst thing a magician can hear after asking the spectator "Was that the card you were thinking of?" is "Sorry, I can't remember!", and in a live theatre show in front of 2000 people this cannot be allowed to happen. This means that the methods being used must be bombproof. And the easy way to do that is to keep it simple!

As we left the theatre in Liverpool, one audience member asked his friend, "How could Derren have predicted the volunteer would have picked 21?" His friend replied that if you ask someone to pick a number between one and a hundred, chances are they will pick 21. I don't believe that for a second and although there are psychological forces that can work, there's too much left to chance to do this in front of a crowd. It's far easier to forget the psychological principles and invoke magician's principles instead. Ask the volunteer to pick a number between one and a hundred, then when they tell you their choice, secretly write it using a tiny hidden pencil attached to your thumb, then reveal your "prediction" that was actually written after the free choice.

For Derren Brown, performing to massive crowds every night, nothing can be left to chance. This is why some of the methods described here may be simpler that you may imagine. Later in the book we'll discuss how an audience member's Grandmother's name was found to be engraved onto a coin which was wrapped inside a ball of wool, in a wineglass, in a locked box. Some of the audience members in Liverpool were discussing having coins that were engraved with every elderly ladies name they could think of, as if that was feasible! The trick needs to work no matter what name is suggested by the audience member, so why not simply engrave the coin live, backstage after the volunteer has told you the name? It's easier and guaranteed to be correct. So why risk anything going wrong? The simplicity of the methods may feel disappointing, but remember – he fooled you and you enjoyed it. That's all that matters.

Beethoven's Piano.

Imagine you've no idea what a piano is. One day, a friend invites you out to see something they know you will love. You arrive at the theatre and watch a two hour show where Beethoven performs all his best work. He's on fire tonight, and the audience loves every moment. On the way out of the theatre, a street trader is selling a book called "Beethoven Exposed – How to play the piano". You buy the book; you buy a piano, and start learning. The book contains all the information on how Beethoven plays the piano, but you can't make it sound like he does. So what do you do next? You keep learning. You practice, you read other books, you buy the DVDs and by putting in the hours you learn your own style. Who knows, maybe one day you will be famous like the man who inspired you, but right now knowing the mechanics isn't enough – you have to put in the practice and learn to be a performer.

It's for this reason that I realise this book will not be for everyone, nor is it supposed to be. Just as buying a Jamie Oliver cook book won't give you the *talent* of a world class chef, knowing the methods of such an outstanding performer risks reducing the content into puzzle solving. We know that a magician does not really saw a woman in half. We suspend our disbelief and enjoy the show. If I tell you there's a trick method involved, have I really told you anything you didn't know?

So who is this book aimed at? I hope that people who read this book are people with a desire to learn showmanship. People who are interested in the art of magic, looking for a way in to learn the craft for themselves. In understanding the methods used, I believe it becomes obvious what a significant part showmanship and presentation have to play to make the trick into a performance. I want up and coming amateur magicians to stop obsessively practicing highly technical moves and techniques, to come out from the bedroom or magic club and work on their personality and performance. Work on being natural, funny, entertaining. Stop learning yet another way to locate a spectator's card in the pack and come up with a new and exciting way to entertain the audience using your own style to make that audience love you.

As I write this, the magic scene in theatre and on television has come back into favour. For the kids, CBBC's 'Help! My Supply Teacher is Magic' combines big illusions with simple tricks you can learn at home. Dynamo has filmed the last episodes of his Magician Impossible series and is touring theatres for the first time. Derren Brown's Infamous has been released on DVD and Miracle has been shown on television. There's never been a better time to see magic, to be inspired by magic and to get involved. If you feel you would like to become a magician, research magic books, join your local club, learn some methods but please remember the most important thing. The audience isn't there to see trickery or be tricked. The audience comes to see *you*. You are the performer, the entertainer. Sure, you can do these feats of magic, but *you* are at the heart of what they see and it's *you* that takes a magic show and turns it into a world class performance.

Magical Thinking.

The common personality trait I see in the most successful magicians is the ability to think magically. This is when a performer takes their well-honed skills and ideas and converts them into something that is real magic in the mind of the spectator. Magical thinking is especially important when keeping the method simple. Magical thinking turns the mundane into the miracle and places the focus on the presentation of magic, not the performance of a trick. In order to demonstrate the power of magical thinking I'd like to use an example where I was completely fooled by a magician myself.

 Many of the top magicians reveal their methods in print and on video, and these are often sold through magic dealers and conventions. It is easy to watch a performance and learn the routine, but it is also easy to fall into the trap of simply impersonating the performer rather than using the knowledge shared to help craft your own style. Many magicians prefer to learn from books for this reason. Books present the ideas and methods but without seeing the performance in action you are left to come up with the presentation yourself. The process of learning from a DVD easily becomes a lesson in mimicking the magician rather than learning.

This is one of the reasons that I do not recommend trying to learn magic from YouTube videos on the internet, as so many of these clips feature badly performed tricks that rely on the reveal of the secret for their popularity. The learning objective for a magician is in taking the secret method and adapting it into a performance that allows them to express their own personality. Magical thinking is the key to this.

I was fooled by a performance that started with a volunteer being picked from the audience. They were handed a pack of cards and the magician explained the three most important things to check when playing cards, especially when in the company of a magician. The first point is that it is important that the deck is a regular deck of fifty two playing cards. There should be no duplicate cards.

The next point was that the cards should not be marked. The magician explained that in a deck of cards the design on the back is identical on every card. In a marked deck there is a secret marking on the back of each card to tell the magician what the card is. Magicians use a technique called the 'Animation Test' to check for marked cards. If the deck is held is a squared block and flicked through from front to back any markings on the cards are easily visible as they flicker and animate whilst the rest of the card design looks solid. The performer rotated the cards and did the same actions on the other half of the back design, explaining that sometimes the marks are only on one half of the cards. The spectator agrees that the cards are not marked.

The magician continued by explaining point number three - the cards must be in a random order. This is extremely important. The best way to do this is to spread the cards all over the table surface, swish them all around, and do this for as long as it takes for you to be happy that the cards are mixed. Then the cards can be pushed back together to reform the deck.

The magician then proceeded to perform a thirty minute routine which in my mind was a collection of incredible feats of memory. The spectator was asked to remove a card and the performer identified which card was missing by spreading the remaining fifty one cards on the table. The spectator was invited to time how long this feat of skill would take, and the magician identified the missing card in only 15 seconds. The performer expressed his disappointment, explaining that the world record for this was 12 seconds and he was so close, yet still unable to beat the record.

The performer then explained that in the process of the previous routine he had now memorised the order of the deck, and proceeded to perform a number of feats of memory. A card was removed from the deck and replaced in a different position, with the magician identifying the card by looking at the spread. The spectator was asked to give a number between one and fifty two, and the performer named the card at that position in the deck. The magic routines kept on coming and I was left with no uncertainty. He had a gift, a talent to remember the order of an entire deck of cards in seconds. At times in the routine I could hear him muttering under his breath, "Katie Holmes, Sven Goran, Caveman", and as I have read up about memory techniques I realised that the performer was using something called memory-palaces, a technique I have studied but never managed to use effectively. Perhaps Katie Holmes must be the initials KH, which might refer to the King of Hearts. Sven Goran is probably code for the Seven of something, and caveman must be a club, right? Even with my educated guesses, I was still impressed that he had managed to use the memory-palaces method to remember an entire pack of cards in 14 seconds. I was blown away by the whole routine.

It's the difference between simply performing a trick and totally mesmerising an audience that promotes a magician from mere entertainer to world-class performer. The magical thinking evident in this routine lifted it from simple card trickery to an incredible feat of mental dexterity. After the performance I spoke to the magician and we discussed his methods. **The entire routine was**

performed using a marked deck. I knew that the feats of "memory" that were being performed would be easy if a marked deck was used, but I was thrown off the scent because the performer had demonstrated at the beginning of the trick that the deck was not marked. He'd even performed the 'Animation Test' to the spectator on both ends of the cards. I still didn't believe him. I figured that he was fobbing me off and didn't want to reveal his actual methods to me, but he went on to explain his magical thinking.

He's a magician. I'm a magician. The volunteer isn't a magician. The spectator is out of their comfort zone just by being on stage. The magician always chooses a spectator from the crowd that isn't holding their hand in the air, or showing any sign that they want to be involved. The animated character reaching their hand high into the air and screaming "pick me!" is going to be a nightmare if they get up on stage. The volunteer is selected from the people who look like they will join in and play along, but won't be too over-enthusiastic or try to deliberately give the performer a hard time.

Remember the introduction to the trick, where the performer explained three things you need to know about cards? He asked the volunteer to check all the cards are different. They can do that, it's easy. Then we show them that the cards are not marked. We show them the

Animation Test. The spectator has no idea what we're talking about. They nod and agree that the cards are probably not marked. The magician can see that the marks on the cards are flashing and flickering all over place, but our spectator doesn't know where to look and does not notice. They trust the magician that the cards are not marked. After all, what kind of idiot magician would be showing us a marked deck, explaining how to see the marks and demonstrating the cards are unmarked, using a marked deck all along? Even magicians are fooled by this approach because they assume that by showing the cards and explaining the 'Animation Test' that the cards cannot possibly be marked so they don't look that closely themselves. The balls-out confidence to pull off an outright lie like this is breathtaking. The magician moves on to point number three, and explains the cards need to be well mixed. The spectator realises that this is back in the comfort zone once more and they will be able to do this. We've moved away from all that marked card nonsense, and are back in familiar territory.

With the idea that the cards are marked completely debunked, the routine appears to be an act of massive skill. The brief mention that a world record for card memorisation exists makes the audience excited for the performer who may be on track to beat the record. The frustration we see increases the belief that the performer is doing something of real skill. Is there really a world record for memorising cards or is this whole thing simply showmanship? His muttering of apparent code words (Katie Holmes = King of Hearts) further cements into the audiences minds that they are seeing something that probably takes many years of practice to learn, when in reality the codes mean nothing.

To compare a routine like this to the sort of tricks I always associated with a marked deck was phenomenal. A lesser performer would ask the spectator to remove a card, and then the magician would name the card they selected, probably by holding a hand to their forehead and acting like they were reading minds or whatever. The routine would be over in a couple of minutes and the audience member would think afterwards, "I wonder if he used a marked deck". After all, marked decks can be bought from toy shops and the general public are familiar with the idea. This routine took the basic premise of a marked deck, and through very talented use of magical thinking dressed up the performance so that the cards themselves were nothing of interest and all focus was on the incredible skill of the performer.

Magical thinking is everything in creation of a performance. Magical thinking takes a great deal of skill and ingenuity, but lifts a magic trick performance to the heights of something you will remember forever. Derren Brown's live shows take the concept of magical thinking beyond anything I have ever seen by other magicians. Please keep this in mind when reading the explanations of the live shows later in this book. By merely explaining the mechanics I wish to convey the incredible artistry on display. Magic secrets are often interesting to know, but the thought processes that take those ideas and make them something so much bigger is what takes some magicians to Vegas whilst others never graduate from table hopping in restaurants.

Finding the Method.

To understand the logic of how a trick works, we need to look at the facts of the performance and focus on the truth of what we have seen, ignoring the parts where your brain fills in the gaps. As a magician, I often hear spectators and volunteers discussing the trick they just saw with friends later and they often describe seeing something that simply didn't happen. The magic takes place in the minds of the audience, and it's easy to think that we saw something that didn't really happen. When we see the magician pass an object from one hand to the other we assume all is above board, but there's every chance that the magician performed the appropriate gestures whilst stealing the object away or retaining it in the same hand. The smallest movement can mask the biggest secrets.

TV magic is often difficult to work out because the director and magician will create the performance together ensuring that the camera follows the ideal audience viewpoint. The direction of the show mimics the misdirection intended by the performer. The live performance of magic is the only real opportunity to see magic unfiltered. Even whilst claiming there are no camera tricks used, an audience reaction shot can be inserted to ensure the home viewer cannot freeze frame and rewind to see the secret moves.

To understand the mindset required in working out a method, I'd like to use a card trick that was shown to me by my grandfather when I was very young. He presented the trick to me and challenged me to work it out. It took a while, but I managed by focussing on what we did know to be true, and puzzling out the rest. I present this to you now so you may try to work it out as well.

Take a deck of cards and remove any nine cards. Mix them up and place three piles of cards on the table, with three cards in each pile. Now play the role of the spectator and choose one of the piles. Lift a pile and turn it over to reveal the bottom card. Remember this card.

Now take all three piles and put them back together to make one pile of nine cards. In doing so, make sure the pile you chose ends up on top, which will make your card the third card from the top in the pile. Now, we will explain to the audience that we are going to perform a spelling trick.

"Magic! M.A.G.I.C, this is going to be magic. Are you ready?"

Now deal the cards onto the table one at a time, spelling the value of the card. For example, if the card was a seven, you would deal S.E.V.E.N, dealing one card for each letter. When you have done this put the remaining pile from your hand on top of the pile on the table. Pick up the whole pile and repeat, this time spelling O.F, dealing two cards. Then again place the remaining cards in your hand on top of the pile on the table, pick up the whole lot, and deal the suit. For example H.E.A.R.T.S, deals five cards one at a time. Put the rest of the cards in your hand on top, pick it all up, and tell the audience that you promised them some real magic, and then spell out M.A.G.I.C. Turn over the card on "C" and it will be the chosen card. How on earth can that possibly be?

Let's now look at the facts of the performance to work out the method.

First of all, the trick just worked, there were no funny moves and no sleights of hand used. The only thing the performer needed to remember was to ensure the chosen card was third from the top when the nine card deck was reassembled. A good way to begin puzzling this out is to turn the chosen card face up so we can easily see where the card is in the deck at any time. For this example, let us pretend you have picked the ace of clubs and this is now in the third position from the top.

The first thing you will do is deal three cards onto the table, (A, C, E). This reverses the order of those three cards. Then you place the remaining cards on top. We are now left with a situation where the order of the first three cards has been reversed, but the remaining cards were not. Your chosen card is now third from the bottom of the deck.

The next thing to do is to pick up the pile and deal the top two cards onto the table (O,F), and then drop the rest of the pack on top. Again, this reverses the order of the two cards, but does not change the order of those that were not dealt. Your card is now 5th from the top.

Finally the cards are picked up again and we deal five cards (C.L.U.B.S). Your card will still be 5th from the top. This means when we deal M.A.G.I.C the last card dealt will be your card.

But how can this trick work? What we do know is that the trick can be performed with a regular deck of cards. We know any nine cards can be chosen. We know that when we copy the magician's performance the routine still works. And we know the trick works with any card chosen. So let's go back and play with this until we work out the magic behind the effect.

In stage one of the trick when we spelled ACE, we dealt three cards onto the table and our card ended up third from the bottom. If we spelled TWO, the order of the cards would have been the same. SIX or TEN also leaves the deck in the same position. Spelling any value will involve dealing at least 3 cards (to spell ACE, ONE, TWO,

SIX, TEN), 4 cards (spelling FOUR, FIVE, NINE), 5 cards (THREE or EIGHT) or 6 cards (to spell SEVEN). Whichever value of card you spell to will only disturb the order of the cards above your chosen card which does not affect the trick because your card will always remain third from the bottom. No numbers have less than three letters when spelled out, JACK, QUEEN and KING also fulfil the requirement so your chosen card will always end in the same position in the deck.

Step two is always the same as you always spell the same word, "OF", leaving your card in the fifth position.

Step 3 is again just more of the same because as long as the word you spell to has 5 or more letters, you will only be disturbing the order of the cards above your card in the deck and your card will always be fifth from the top at the end. Whether you spell CLUBS, HEARTS, SPADES or DIAMONDS does not matter, as each of those options has enough letters. This means that when you spell MAGIC, the C will always be the chosen card.

By experimenting with different spellings and keeping watch on the position of the chosen card it is easy to see how it works. By focussing on what we know to be factual, ignoring the magicians patter about his apparent powers, we concentrate on what we can see and solve the puzzle.

Wait – didn't we already say that magic should be more than just a puzzle to be solved? The secret is just the mechanics, and now we can improve this trick with a little magical thinking. For example, if we know the name of the spectator, how many letters are in their name? Can we spell their name instead of MAGIC at the end? If their name is Steven, can we call them Steve? Can we use a personal five letter word for the last stage of the trick? Instead of spelling magic, we can spell to something more personal. How about spelling "David is amazing" instead of seven of clubs? That becomes a bigger mind-bender. A simple trick goes a long way when combined with amazing presentation and magical thinking, and the further away you get from the facts of the performance, the harder it becomes to work out the method.

<u>Bringing it all Together.</u>

Let's examine a routine that uses everything we have covered so far, combining a simple mind reading effect, but adding a multiple out, a bit of magical thinking and some extra presentation. Derren Brown's "Smoke" routine is a great example of how to present yourself as a master of your craft.

We start with a traditional magic trick, in this case the "Mind Power Deck", a gimmicked pack of cards available from magic dealers. Many years ago, I purchased a trick called Hallucination from Steven Tucker Magic which uses a similar principle. You can even make a deck by purchasing multiple regular packs of cards and constructing it yourself. The "Mind Power Deck" from Penguin Magic takes the principle a stage further and is the version I recommend. The trick is based around the way that we behave when we choose a card from a deck. If a pack of cards is spread face up in a ribbon across the table and we are asked to pick one, we will focus our attention on the card we choose to pick, and not worry too much about the other cards. This is where the Mind Power deck comes in. Whilst there are 52 cards spread onto the table, the deck is made up of a sequence of 6 cards, repeated many times over. The deck I made consists of a low, medium and high value card in red and the same again in black. When the cards are spread and the spectator is asked to choose one, their eyes dart over the cards, and they focus on the one they want to pick. As far as they are concerned they are looking at 52 different cards. The red and black colours further assist the illusion of a full, regular deck of cards. When the spectator makes a choice we know it's one of only 6 cards.

There are many tricks that involve a magician indentifying a chosen card but the beauty of this approach is that the spectator merely chooses a card in their mind, with no need to physically pick the card out and replace it in the deck. The basic mind read routine would go like this:

"I want you to look into the cards as I spread them, pick one card in your mind, and don't tell me, don't point at the card or give me any clues, just look into the pack and choose a card" (instructing the spectator to look "into" the pack forces the spectator to actually look – otherwise they may just choose their favourite card, the one they always pick, and in this routine we need to be sure that they choose one of the six cards available).

"What I would like you to do now is to focus your mind on the card. Keep saying the name of the card to yourself in your mind. OK. I am starting to see the card you are thinking of – I believe your card is a red card".

If the spectator agrees, then the first part is done. If they disagree, the magician can make a joke by showing the backs of the cards and saying, "Look, they are all red!" I feel this is cheeky, but you get away with it. It feels a bit clunky to me though, and I'm glad you only need to do this 50% of the time!

Now we know the spectator has chosen a black card. The three black cards in the deck are a two, a Queen and a seven, and the magician quickly asks a cleverly worded question.

"It's not a high card is it?"

This question is positioned with a tone of voice that pitches it halfway between a question and a statement, and the words can be taken two ways by the spectator. The spectator's response will be a firm yes or no if the card is the Queen or the two. There will be uncertainty in the response if the card is the seven. Either way, the magician knows the chosen card now, and can reveal this information as part of a demonstration of their mind reading ability.

That's quite a nice trick, but let's examine how Derren Brown and the team behind the series Mind Control used showmanship, presentation, multiple-outs and magical thinking to bamboozle Stephen Fry when they performed the same trick.

Instead of using just any deck containing six repeating cards, the Mind Power deck was used to add further magical opportunity. In this deck, the value of the card printed at the top left (the card index) does not match the value printed at the bottom right. When the cards are spread on the table from left to right, only the value at the top left is visible on each card, and these corners only show six cards repeating throughout the deck as explained above. The magician asks the spectator to look into the deck and choose a card. However, when the cards are scooped back up, the pack can be rotated 180 degrees and when spread on the table a second time the visible values are those from the opposite corner. This now appears to be a genuine spread of 52 different cards. In a beautiful piece of magical thinking the apparent 52 cards you can see do not match any of the 6 cards printed on the opposite corners, allowing the performer to show that the chosen card was never in the deck in the first place. Derren uses this to his advantage later on in the routine.

Now, we need to use magical thinking to try and improve the slightly clumsy questioning that is to follow. We ask the spectator to think about the name of the card in their mind, but we will use a subtlety to give us the chance of a miracle early on in the routine. One of the cards in the selection of six choices is the King of Hearts. Being a picture card and brightly coloured it's an easy card for the eyes to rest upon. This card is the one out of six that gets picked most often and this can be used to the magician's advantage by adding this into the dialogue as follows.

"So I want you to think about the card you have chosen, don't say the name of the card out loud, just say it to yourself, over and over again like this.... King of Hearts, King of Hearts, King of Hearts."

It's at this point in the routine that Stephen Fry shouts out, *"Oh fuck off!"*

Stephen is blown away because Derren really did just read his mind! We know however that this is a great combination of presentation, magical thinking and multiple-outs. Stephen Fry really had chosen the King of Hearts and so a real miracle just occurred and there is a one in six chance of that miracle happening in every performance. However, if Stephen had picked one of the other five cards then the words that Derren had said simply sound like instructions to be followed and the King of Hearts is merely being used as an example of how to say the name of the card over in your mind. Then Derren would have continued in the style of the first version of the trick that we covered earlier, suggesting that the card is a RED card and using whatever questions he would have used in the less impressive presentation of the routine.

Derren is smoking throughout this performance, and Stephen Fry, still reeling from having his mind read is told that there's something strange going on. Did he really see a King of Hearts in the deck? Derren explains that the cards have been in full view throughout but there isn't a King of Hearts in the pack. The cards are now ribbon spread onto the table, and sure enough, as the pack has been rotated 180 degrees, the visible card indexes show an apparent full deck with no King of Hearts. No-one would ever notice that there are another five cards also missing – to any spectator this is a regular deck with only one card missing. And throughout the routine, Derren is smoking, so his reach for a cigarette pack in his inside pocket seems incidental, throwaway, nothing to see here.

In fact, the cigarette pack is the vital prop to the climax of the trick, as it contains six rolled up cards where the cigarettes should be. As soon as Derren knows the chosen card, he can remove a cigarette from the box which is actually one of the six cards inside the cigarette box. Derren chooses the card that matches Stephen's choice and switches it for the real cigarette on an off-beat. This provides a great ending to the effect as the card has apparently disappeared from the deck and is now on fire in Derren's mouth.

Showmanship, magical thinking and performance, combined with an amazing gimmicked deck of cards created an incredible magic routine which Stephen Fry will remember for the rest of his life. Would the reaction have been the same if Derren had simply performed the trick with the gimmicked deck as per the instruction booklet? Again, the presentation lifts the routine to world class, even though at the heart is a trick deck that anyone could perform.

The Methods Revealed in this Book

In a TV special, 'Derren Brown – The Events', Derren muttered the magic words "Big Bang, Alakazam" during a trick where a light bulb powered up and then exploded whilst inside a clear plastic bag. The magic dealer Alakazam sell a prop that looks exactly like this effect, and the trick happens to be called 'Big Bang". Does this mean that Derren Brown was using a store bought trick on stage? In my opinion, yes. He gives a cheeky nod to any magicians watching and I chuckled at the audacity of naming the trick on TV during the performance. But can I prove this was the exact method used? No – Derren happened to say the name of a magic dealer and one of the tricks they sell, whilst performing a trick that looked exactly like it. That could still be, however unlikely, a coincidence. Derren Brown and his team are very tight-lipped about the actual methods they use, and there's no way I could get any confirmation that the methods I reveal are the actual methods he uses.

In my work as a magician and magic dealer, I attend conventions and shows where magic apparatus is sold. Magic methods are discussed openly. Derren is very clear in every performance where he explains his effects are achieved with a combination of magic, suggestion, psychology, misdirection and showmanship.

During the FISM International World Championships of Magic in 2012, I saw 150 performers over seven days, showing off their stage acts in the hope of winning the competition. One act started his performance by walking onto the stage wearing a top hat and tails. He made doves appear apparently from nowhere. Each time a new dove appeared he walked over to an ornate wooden table and placed the bird on a perch. By the end of the act there must have been ten birds on the perch. For his finale, he walked over to the birds, covered them with a silk cloth, whipped the cover away and the birds had disappeared. The trick was impressive and I enjoyed the performance. Later in the day another magician started their performance by walking onto the stage towards a table, suspiciously looking like this was the exact same table. Of course this probably means that both magicians had bought the same magic gimmicked table, maybe even from the same dealer. An experienced magician begins to recognise certain props and now I know that this performer is probably going to make some doves appear, because this table will be instrumental in making them disappear again at the end of the act. I don't know the exact make and model of the table, but I've seen four magicians using it since then, and every time the magician places birds on a perch, then they disappear. I can say with absolute certainty that this table is the key to the routine as it's too much of a coincidence that all the dove magicians I saw use it. The prop table must have some mechanism that allows the doves to be quickly concealed inside. The more magicians I see performing, the more I see props like this on stage. So now, before a magician has even started the show I know that if I see that table on stage, he's likely to make doves appear and disappear by magic.

Does this mean the magicians were absolutely without question using this method? No, we cannot prove anything. Is it extremely likely that the table is a specific prop for making doves vanish? Yes, it surely has to be. It's too much of a coincidence that all the dove magicians happened to purchase the same table because it looks nice – it's a special dove table.

So when, in the Infamous stage show, Derren brings out a book of The Complete Works of Shakespeare, do I assume this to be just a regular book from a bookstore? The audience does. But when I know that I have seen a book that looks exactly like the one he uses for sale at a Magic Convention, where the book is specially manufactured to allow exactly that same effect to be performed, does that mean I know Derren's Brown's method? No, I cannot prove that. But it is likely that he's using the trick book? Yes, I think so.

So, I won't be possible for me to say these methods are absolutely without question the methods used on stage by Derren and his team. The methods that follow are those that I would use if I wanted to perform the same effect. However, I have the confidence that these are the methods Derren is using and if not, I believe the correct method will be similar. As we've already covered, in a live environment with 1000 people watching, I'd certainly choose the easiest method I can come up with, and I've spent a number of years researching approaches that I believe cannot fail.

And what of psychic ability and mind reading? Again, if Derren is using these techniques (despite his proclamations that he is not!) then he's definitely doing it the hard way. It's possible that someone with Derren's extraordinary skill-set could memorise the first line of every page of the complete works of Shakespeare. But what's the point if you can buy a gimmicked book that does the work for you?

The content and format of this book.

Derren Brown's live shows run for around two and a half hours with a short interval. When televised they come in around an hour and thirty minutes with breaks for advertisements. I have personally attended every live show he has performed, apart from The Gathering (a specially invited mix of celebrity audience members and the public) and Something Wicked This Way Comes. My fascination in learning the methods came from An Evening of Wonders in Carlisle, where Derren performed what he calls the 'Oracle Act', a demonstration of mind reading which revealed specific information about audience members. I felt there was no way he could have done this without stooges in the audience. My friends and I went to see the show again in Blackpool and this showed us there were no stooges and no repeated information. We even checked the cards and envelopes for gimmicks and found nothing. We were fooled – we had simply no idea how it was done. The following year the Enigma show simply blew us away and to this day it remains my favourite Derren Brown live show. Svengali and Infamous were also amazing shows, with each having its own theme and tone, despite all the shows being magic and mentalism based. I've been disappointed that in some of the TV transmissions they have missed out sequences that I found to be the most memorable, but in writing this book I decided to follow the TV and DVD versions of the live shows. I believe this to be the best way to provide structure to the book and for the reader to be able to revisit the performance with new knowledge of my methods.

For example, when I researched the Oracle Act, my initial guesses involved incredible effort and subterfuge on the part of Derren's team to find out the secrets of the audience members. My initial method involved looking up ticket reservations, names on credit cards, Facebook and so on. When I discovered what I believe to be the actual method, it was so simple that I didn't believe it. It took re-watching the DVD to make me realise that the method worked and was a hundred times simpler than I had imagined it would be.

We'll take the recorded performances in order of release starting with Something Wicked This Way Comes, continue into Evening of Wonders, Enigma, Svengali and Infamous, ending with Miracle. I'll include a discussion of Underground and Secret, although these are "best of" shows which consist of content from the previous shows already covered. I will not include The Gathering as this was made for television and all the shows I will focus on in this book are those that I have witnessed live. At the time of writing, the last filmed show, Miracle, has been shown on TV, and Underground / Secret is concluding its UK run.

An explanation of pre-show work and 'Dual Reality'

Pre-show work and Dual Reality are amazing tools for a magician to use in a live environment. Pre-show work involves asking a volunteer if they will take part in the show before it starts. Conversation will involve the content of the show. The magician may ask the volunteer if they have a favourite name, for example. They will ask what it is, and explain that it's great that they have a favourite name because one of the tricks in the show involves favourite names. The magician will ask the volunteer if they are willing to take part in the show later, *"we'll use that name in one of the tricks"*. The volunteer does not realise that this preparation is going to create a different effect for the audience.

Dual Reality also involves the magician performing the trick to a spectator on stage. The spectator is not a stooge and is not 'in' on the trick. Through use of language and the audience's perception of events, two tricks are performed simultaneously, with a major effect and a minor effect taking place. The spectator on stage takes part in the routine and sees the events from their own point of view. They forget that the audience has their own perspective on the show and don't realise that the audience is seeing something that appears much bigger and more impressive than the actual events happening. For example, the volunteer may be asked to *"choose any word"*. The audience cannot see that there is a list of five words to choose from. The list is in plain sight of the volunteer. By the end of the routine the volunteer is impressed that the mind reader could know which word was chosen from the list, but the audience believes the volunteer could have thought of any totally random word. Dual Reality effects can sometimes be spotted by noting the disparity between the audience reaction and the volunteer reaction.

I saw a great example of Dual Reality when I first started to learn magic in the early 1990s. Three volunteers were invited to draw a picture and were given a large square of cardboard each. They were instructed to imagine their picture in as large, colourful and clear a way as they could, then they were invited to draw their image on their piece of card. The audience at this point think the volunteers can be drawing anything they choose, but they do not realise that on each card, written in light pencil to prevent the audience seeing it, there is already an instruction to the artist regarding their image. This could say "You are player one, your image is a HOUSE." The next card could say "You are player two, your image is a FISH". The language used by the magician refers to the drawings as *"your image"* and the volunteer sees nothing unusual about this because they do not know what the end result of the trick is going to be. They simply follow the instructions they are given. The cards are then placed in envelopes, which are secretly marked so the performer can tell which envelope contains which image. As the climactic moment to the performance arrives the magician uses all his acting skills to suggest that he his using his mind reading powers to determine the contents of the first envelope. He explains his thought processes:

"I'm getting the sensation of an image created by someone with a great sense of fun in their lives. I think this is someone who has a number of important decisions to be made at the moment, and someone who is looking to travel soon. The way they have drawn the image tells me they feel they should be more organised in their life. I think this image was drawn by our volunteer Amanda, and this is a picture of a... mouse! "

The envelope is dramatically opened and revealed to show the image was indeed drawn by the named volunteer and was a mouse as predicted. This reveal is repeated for each volunteer. They all believe that the trick has been a success as the magician knew it was their picture, even though it was sealed in an envelope. Also the cold-reading statements regarding the volunteer's lifestyle (statements that apply to everyone – the examples I used above would pretty much apply to anyone in the demographic of that volunteer) add further distraction from the overall method. Each volunteer saw one main miracle, which was that the magician knew which envelope contained their image.

The audience however saw a much bigger picture. They cannot understand how the magician knew what was inside the envelope, which volunteer drew the image and what the image would be. The audience don't know that the volunteers were instructed to draw specific items, and as far as they are concerned the three of them had a free choice to draw anything in the world that they wanted to.

Dual reality can be combined with pre-show work with unbelievable results. In our example, the magician could ask the audience member to draw a picture, and write their favourite name underneath the drawing. Then the magician can reveal an envelope that was clearly in view on stage the whole time, and open it up to reveal his 'prediction' of a picture of a house with the name written underneath. The volunteer doesn't realise that the audience sees the "favourite name" as an extra piece of mind reading, because the audience was not privy to the pre-show conversation.

 There is no way I could possibly know what was discussed privately before a show with a potential volunteer. Pre-show work is an incredible tool for the mentalism performer and can be used to dazzling effect in the right environment. I cover it here because I believe the Oracle Act uses elements of Pre-show in its method.

Finally, it's worth having a brief explanation of what magicians call "Instant Stooging", although this is a technique that I do not like to use for reasons that will become obvious. Instant Stooging is one step away from using an actual stooge, and is akin to a hypnotist whispering to a volunteer, *"just play along mate and I'll slip you a tenner after the show"*. With Instant Stooging the volunteer becomes a willing participant in the deception of the audience. For example a volunteer could be asked to choose a random page from a paperback book, but when they look inside each page has "choose page 146" written in thick marker pen. On page 146 further instructions could be written. The volunteer, in front of a whole audience and now part of the show simply has no choice but to play along.

Very strong and powerful magic can be achieved through Instant Stooging but it is bad form for magicians to use this technique because the volunteer will ultimately return to their friends in the audience and explain the method to them. Dual Reality is a far better process because everyone feels like they experienced the magic, whilst Instant Stooging can be ruined by the secrets being shared immediately afterwards. This can seriously harm a performer's reputation, especially if they spent the whole show hyping themselves up as an accomplished wizard, demonstrating their skills and achievements in mentalism only for their volunteer to give all the tricks away as soon as they leave the stage. A magician of Derren Brown's ability would steer clear of Instant Stooging, but it's an interesting area for further reading.

Watching Derren Brown Performances.

My recommendation would be to buy the DVD box set of the live shows and view them in the correct order. These shows have also appeared on the All4 On-Demand service, although this changes from time to time. I would watch the performance in full, then read the methods, and watch again, reading along as you go. I will reveal my theories and methods for the tricks seen in the filmed theatre shows so the layout of the chapters of the book will match the running order allowing you to read along as you rewatch. The shows in sequence are Something Wicked This Way Comes, Evening of Wonders, Enigma, Infamous, Miracle and Underground (also known as Secret). As far as I am aware, the first show, Derren Brown Live, isn't available to purchase and The Gathering involved a celebrity audience which may or may not suggest the involvement of pre-show work. I will focus on the DVDs in the box set and also Infamous which is released on DVD separately. The TV broadcast of Miracle excluded one of my favourite routines, and I will include this also in case it is released as a DVD extra. Finally, if you have the opportunity to see Secret / Underground while they are still playing, you really should!

Something Wicked This Way Comes.

The show.

Something Wicked This Way Comes is the first show we can buy on DVD for review. As one of his earliest performances (Derren Brown Live was the first theatre show and this has never been released for sale) it demonstrates a wider repertoire of skills than the work Derren is best known for. Sections of this show would come under the Circus Skills category in my view, and whilst it is still fantastic all the way through, it's the phenomenal ending routine with newspapers that fits the typical Derren Brown style. Later shows relied less on traditional performance art (walking on glass, nails in the nose, card routines etc.) and are more magic based, but this is still an amazing performance and if you have never seen it before, you should stop reading now and watch the DVD without the distraction of this book.

Introduction.

The show begins with a volunteer picked from the audience by throwing a toy monkey around to demonstrate that the choice is random. As always this really is random, and Derren never uses stooges in the live shows. Derren asks the volunteer to choose an animal, and makes jokes that he will not "lead" the volunteer into suggesting a particular animal, he'd have to be "barking" mad to say that! He continues this theme and within the banter he tells the volunteer that they should not choose a dog, cat or monkey, fish or bird. Or a cow. This takes all the usual choices out of the equation, and the volunteer picked a mouse. Most people will pick Elephant, and Derren comments on this to the audiences agreement (a classic trick called the "Elephants in Denmark" trick is a really simple suggestive force which shows that if you ask people to think of an animal that begins with an E, and a country beginning with D, they will almost always say Elephants in Denmark), but the volunteer chose mouse, and the show continues with the volunteer, Danni, joining Derren on the stage.

Danni is asked to turn around the card on the stage and there's a crudely drawn picture which gets a laugh from the audience. Danni is given a locked briefcase to keep in her care throughout the show when she returns to the audience. Danni is also given an envelope to keep and Derren takes an item of jewellery from Danni which is taken backstage.

Danni opens the envelope that was underneath the case on the table, and the envelope contains a prediction of the animal Danni chose. It is worth noting here is that a lot has happened onstage as a distraction around this prediction. Watching the DVD, Danni says "mouse" for the first time at 5 minutes and 6 seconds into the performance. Meanwhile, the lights are low and it would be easy for a stagehand to put the prediction envelope in place by entering the stage hiding behind the card with the question mark on it. There is a 30 second window where the lights remain low and no-one approaches this setup on the stage until 6m 35 seconds – that's over a minute and a half to get the envelope in place. Since Derren explained that Danni must not choose cat, monkey, dog, cow and so on earlier, it's likely that backstage there is a selection of prediction envelopes with the most common choices pre-printed. I'd expect there's also a computer to print a bespoke prediction should the volunteer pick an animal they have not be printed. If you want to see exactly how the stagehand gets on the stage behind the question mark card, watch the extra features on the DVD. At the start of backstage documentary there is a time-lapse film of the stage setup. Pause this and go through frame by frame, you will clearly see the hidden door in the background, open all the way through the latter half of the time-lapse. So this first trick is easy to do, the prediction envelope is simply placed onto the stage after the prediction is made.

Spot the Liar.

Earlier in the book, I explained about the presentation being the key to the performance. If there was ever a trick in Derren's shows that demonstrates presentation over method this is it. I explained earlier how I hope that anyone reading this book with a view to enhancing their magical knowledge takes away the message that the presentation and performance are the most important things. I have seen and spoken to many magicians over the years that forget this and become obsessed with the mechanics of the trick. I have seen a magician who knows hundreds of different ways of locating a spectator's chosen card in the pack, with some of his techniques being so utterly complex they defy explanation. I've also met a magician who only knows one method, a technique so simple that he learned it when he was very young and has continued to use it all his life. However, the latter performer knows hundreds of ways of revealing the spectator's chosen card. He makes it appear inside an orange, stuck inside a car window, or inside the spectator's shoe. He is a wonderful magical thinker and side by side most people would consider him the better magician of the two discussed here. In actual fact the former is simply ridiculously talented, but to the audience he only knows one trick. The methods he uses are incredible but when performed properly magical methods should not be visible at all, and this is where the presentation comes in. So at the risk of sounding like a stuck record, presentation is everything, and nowhere is this demonstrated better than this trick.

Derren Brown asks five audience members to write down the surname of the first person they had a crush on. They are handed a clipboard and pen and they are asked to write large, clear writing. There's a reason for this, which we will come to later.

Derren starts to play the game, "Spot the Liar". He uses a bag containing balls which are picked at random by the volunteers on the stage. Derren asks questions to the volunteers, and asks them to lie if they were given a white ball and tell the truth if they are the one volunteer with the black ball. Derren's patter during the explanation and setup of this game is a really great example of using language to control every element of the routine to make sure nothing can go wrong. For example, he asks the last volunteer to check the bag to ensure there are no balls remaining in the bag. He also explains that white balls mean lie, and the black ball means to tell the truth multiple times to ensure everyone understands the game. You can see from the performance there are no opportunities for one volunteer to select two balls for example.

The presentation of the trick lasts for a good length of time, with Derren using visual clues, body-language and other NLP related techniques to deduce which of the volunteers is lying and which is telling the truth. Or so he would have us believe.

In fact, the method to this trick could be much simpler than that. It all comes down to the most innocuous of details which is the method of choosing who would lie and who would tell the truth. Derren holds the bag with the balls in, and the volunteers remove one ball each. There are four white balls and one black ball and for my method the black ball would be heavier than the white balls. Derren knows from the weight of the bag when someone has taken the black ball out of the bag. From this point on, Derren can present the trick in any way he wishes. He can react to the answers the volunteers give and he can explain the bogus NLP techniques he is apparently using to deduce which volunteer is the liar, because he knows well before the game starts which one has the black ball.

You can see that in the DVD Derren holds the bag whilst the balls are chosen, but once the black ball is chosen he can let go and the final two volunteers pass the bag between themselves.

Derren's team also need to know which volunteer has the black ball, because they need to know which clipboard she was given earlier when they were asked to write the name of their first crush. Derren can write the name of her first crush on his pad by reading her mind. However that is the hard way. There are magic dealers that sell devices known as "magic clipboards" that transmit the image or writing from the clipboard to an iPad or similar device via Bluetooth or Wi-Fi. However, since the clipboards were just seen briefly on stage, no-one in the audience is suspecting the clipboards of being gimmicked in any way. In the eyes of the audience they are a simple utility device for the volunteers to lean on, and no-one pays them any attention at all – why would they? Therefore I suggest this method could be as simple as having a piece of carbon paper on each clipboard. When the volunteers write the names, the clipboards are taken backstage; the required name is noted and placed somewhere for Derren to clearly see. My suggestion is that this would be in the wings of the stage, when he walks to pick up the pen and pad. Once he knows the name, it's easy to present the reveal of this information as if he is reading her body language or thoughts.

Blockhead (or: Hammering a Nail into your Nose)

Before we begin, may I take a moment to impress upon you the importance of not attempting this trick? I have performed this myself many times after a great deal of practice, and whilst the method here is a detailed description of the way I perform it, I must impress upon you not to try this yourself. It could be extremely dangerous!

When people have asked me how it is done, I always ask them how they think it is done. As explained at the beginning of this book, the layperson (non-magician) will often come up with a far more complicated theory than the actual method used. I overheard an audience member speculating about a special magic hammer which trimmed a length from the end of the nail with every tap. The nail would be shown sticking out from the performer's nostril and with every tap of the hammer the nail would get a little shorter. This would give the illusion of the nail going into the nose. For some people, a special kind of magic hammer seems much more plausible than simply believing that what you are seeing is actually what is really happening in front of you.

If you have seen the Derren Brown show, you already know how this trick was performed. In my method there isn't really a secret. The performer takes a nail, a hammer and proceeds to do exactly what you see on the screen. So how does the performer avoid injury?

The most important part of this trick is the preparation. The performer doesn't just nip to his local branch of Homebase and buy a pack of nails. However, in theory that would be OK, as long as the nail was solid steel with no possibility of any rust or other particles at risk of becoming detached during performance. I once read of a magician who tried to learn this trick by using a cotton bud instead of a nail. His idea was that the soft cotton tip would protect his tender nasal cavities from injury. Whilst I agree that a sharp pointed nail seems more dangerous than a cotton bud, the reality is that cotton buds have many tiny fibres that can easily become detached from the head. The last thing you want is a thin, wispy piece of cotton stuck fast on the tissue inside your nose, and this magician surely regretted his impulsive approach to learning the trick. Rather than learning the method properly from an experienced performer, he decided to give it a go in front of the bathroom mirror one boring afternoon, and ended up in hospital having the cotton fibre surgically removed from his nasal cavity after sneezing constantly for almost a week.

So how does our Blockhead (as the trick is known) performer reduce any risk to themselves? There are magic dealers who sell nails (and other similar items, drill-bits etc) designed specifically for the performance of this routine. One dealer describes the nails on his website as follows:

"All blockhead equipment I make is made from 316L grade surgical stainless steel. It is non-magnetic, will never rust on its own, holds a mirror finish and is even surgical implant grade steel. This is the same steel used in skeletal Fixator pins, dental braces, cardiac stents and most commonly in body jewellery. This type of steel is also used industrially in food processing factories for its extreme anti-corrosive qualities. What all this means is, it's GOOD to be in your body!"

So as a performer, you source the correct type of nail, you ensure the nail is kept sterilised and perfectly clean and free from dust and lint. Then during the performance, you safely and gently slide the nail into your nasal cavity. When I perform this routine, I ensure the nail has a large flat protruding end to hammer. This is to prevent the nail from going irretrievably far into the nose. It has to be pulled back out again or that's another trip to the hospital.

As for how the nasal cavity works, here's a simple way to see for yourself how it happens. Most of the time, you have one nostril that feels clearer than the other. It's rare that you feel both nostrils allowing you to breathe as easily as each other. So whilst you sit reading this, close your mouth and take a deep breath in through your nose. You should be able to feel the passage of air entering the nose and going down the throat. That's the same path the nail takes when inserted during this routine. Obviously the nail doesn't go down the throat, but by using the nails specifically made for this trick you can see that the nail simply rests horizontally in the space between the nostril and the back wall of the throat. If the performer can feel the tip of the nail (which must not be sharp of course!) on the back wall of the throat then this nail is too long and could cause injury.

The DVD of this show shows a safety warning at the start, explaining that the performance involves very dangerous tricks that should not be tried at home. The message also explains that the performance was supervised by health and safety professionals, and I would be sure that a performer such as Derren Brown would have the nails specially made to order, made to be exactly the right length and of the correct materials. We also see him wipe the nail with a liquid from a medicinal looking bottle. Whether this is just for show is debatable, but I'd suggest this is some sort of safe cleansing solution to ensure that no injury could occur. And as we end this description, I will just add a final word of warning – don't try this.

Walking on Glass.

There are entire books written on the subject of walking on broken glass, and there would be impractical to try to explain how to walk on broken glass in a book such as this one. If you really want to know all the detail, simply head to your local magic dealer and buy a specific book for this topic. In Derren's performance, two buckets of broken glass are poured out onto the stage. Two bottles are broken on the stage by volunteers. Some have considered that perhaps the glass from the buckets was some sort of fake glass, and the only real glass in this performance is that from the two bottles. Some performers carry glass specifically from one performance to the next. The glass is sharp but the sharpest edges and points are simply filed down to prevent large pieces of glass leaving shards in the skin. The distribution of weight usually means that the performer is not placing enough weight specifically on one piece of glass and this prevents the injury you might expect from watching the performance.

(Fun fact - Derren discusses a performer from the 1930's known as The Great Prestoni. As we will see in other shows, Derren can present stories as fact in order to sell an illusion. Whilst Google doesn't seem to have heard of The Great Prestoni, it's a fun coincidence that Andy Nyman, this show's co-creator, has a son called Preston.)

In order to enter an apparent trance state to allow him to walk on the glass, Derren appears to be able to stop his pulse completely. As with all the methods explained in this book, I cannot say with absolute certainty that the technique I would use is the exact same method that Derren and his team would use. However, the effect of stopping the pulse has been performed by legendary magician David Berglas and I would expect a performer of Derren's calibre to have learned from the best. If I needed to stop my pulse for the purposes of a performance like this, I would conceal a tennis ball or similar item in my armpit. Pressing the arm against my body with the tennis ball in place can restrict the blood flow and temporarily slow the pulse to almost nothing. A nurse, or similar volunteer experienced in taking pulses would be shocked to feel the pulse slowing and apparently stopping.

And once more, a reminder that the purpose of this book is to gain an understanding of the methods to demonstrate the importance of the performance. Don't be smashing bottles on the floor and walking over them. That would be very silly and **extremely dangerous** if you don't know what you're doing. A book like this cannot possibly give you all the information you would need to begin attempting a skill like this.

Counting Buttons.

In another wonderful presentation of a traditional magic trick, Derren talks about developing an ability to make rapid calculations in his head with experiences of pain. He asks the volunteer on the stage to take buttons from a bowl and to put them on a tray. He surprises the volunteer by asking her to slap him. He then reacts by counting the buttons instantly. Of course the pain has nothing to do with the mechanics of the trick. There are a number of ways this effect can be achieved, and I would go for the simplest, using a gimmicked tray or table. The gimmick could be a weighing scale mechanism. There are devices for sale in magic shops that look like very ordinary household items with extraordinary tech built in to them. I've seen cheap looking clipboards that transmit the volunteer's writing to an iPad, dice that transmit their orientation to a receiver that taps the answer against the performer's leg and other items that look ordinary but are anything but. I've also seen an ordinary looking tray that has a weighing scale built in. Derren could see the weight of the bowl with the buttons. He can see the number of buttons that are removed by the weight reading from the mechanism built into the thick wooden table with the bowl on. My method for this performance would involve a readout hidden in the tray. On the DVD, the volunteer makes a mess of removing the red cloth and rotates the tray 90 degrees at the same time. This seems to cause a problem for Derren, and he starts to say that he's not got the answer, then makes a guess anyway. When they sit down he is very specific on the rotation of the tray. When he revises his guess, the tray is facing exactly the same way to him that it would have been if the volunteer had kept the tray in her left hand as instructed. All the performer needs to do is read the information on how many buttons are left, then make a performance to distract from the mechanics and props involved. Derren's face slapping is a brilliant distraction!

Newspaper Test.

Once again Derren performs a routine where the presentation of the trick distracts from an extremely simple method. This trick is one of the best examples of misdirection that I've seen, because the presentation apparently includes the explanation of how it was done! Derren performs an incredible prediction trick then he shows you how he did it using psychology, misdirection and showmanship. The key here is the misdirection. Whilst the prediction is impressive, the explanation of how he did it is even more impressive. The explanation sells the illusion of a huge psychological experiment which shocks and surprises the audience with its complexity. The explanation however is completely bogus, and serves to sell the trick by revealing a method that's a million times more impressive than the actual method.

Throughout this entire section, we need to remember that whatever happens, Derren will reveal at the end of the show that he has been using subliminal clues to influence the audience to choose page 14 of the Daily Mail, and to tear around the word Influential. For my method to work every time, we need to ensure these three random elements (Daily Mail, Page 14, Influential) are forced in apparently free choice situations.

It's worth revisiting the exact sequence of events for this explanation. Derren throws ten newspapers into the audience. The first is a copy of The Times which is deliberately thrown to the front row. The remaining newspapers are thrown out into the audience at random. This process is much more tightly controlled than it would appear as we will see in a moment. Derren invites Danni back onto the stage for the finale of the trick. She's been sat in the audience trying out combinations on the briefcase padlock that she was given at the start of the show, to no avail. In my method, Danni doesn't realise that this is no ordinary padlock but a special gimmicked lock that is available to purchase from magic dealers. The lock has a combination dial which serves as a distraction to another secret mechanism that can be activated by the magician. Danni can't open this lock with any combination when she is in the audience but when she brings it back on stage, the secret mechanism is activated and the lock will now open when any combination is entered.

Derren asks Danni to choose one of the audience members who is holding up their newspaper. She chooses Kirsty, and she happens to be holding the Daily Mail. This is the first of a number of "forces" we will see in my method for this trick. For the finale to work, Danni had to choose an audience member who was holding the Daily Mail. When Derren threw the newspapers into the crowd, most of the newspapers were Daily Mail. He threw a copy of The Times to someone on the front row, and some different newspapers specifically went to the balcony seats and Derren said to pass them further back. The apparently random throwing of newspapers actually distributed multiple copies of the Daily Mail to various seats visible from the stage, a copy of the Times to the very front row, and one or two different papers to seats that would be almost invisible from the stage. Derren is even heard to comment that some of the newspapers are duplicates. This small, throwaway comment stops audience members who may get a glimpse of two identical newspapers from realising that most of the newspapers were the Daily Mail. So, force number one is complete. Our volunteer has picked a random audience member who could have been holding any newspaper, but the visible volunteers all have the Daily Mail, and the trick is well underway.

Next, we need the volunteer to open the briefcase. We know that the special lock means that whatever numbers happen to pop into the volunteer's mind, the case is going to open. So this trick is entirely presentation. The volunteer chooses some random numbers, and the case is opened. Derren does some lovely misdirection here by asking her to change one of the digits of the last number chosen. This sells the illusion that Derren is using his mind techniques to get Danni to guess the correct combination, but really any numbers would have opened the lock. You'll also see Derren ask Kirsty, "you picked the....

Daily?" and Kirsty replies, "Mail!" which again sells the illusion that she could have any of the 10 different newspapers in her hand, where she actually will always have the Daily Mail during every show.

Derren comments that Kirsty is too far away, so he takes a newspaper from someone nearer. This is the copy of The Times we saw earlier, the first newspaper of the pile, deliberately controlled to be thrown to someone in the front row. This is a specially constructed newspaper. The cover is a copy of today's newspaper, but the pages of the newspaper are anything but normal. For my method, I'd take around ten different newspapers and remove page 14 from each. These pages are placed on top of each other and the cover wrapped around them. The result is a newspaper which looks normal, has different headlines on each page, but every left hand page will have the page number 14. Derren reads headlines from left hand pages, slowly so that the volunteer chooses one before Derren reaches the halfway point of the newspaper. This is important because the pages after halfway will be the later page numbers from the other side of the printed sheets. The volunteer says stop, Derren shows her the headline she has chosen and page 14 is always the page number. Danni could have said to stop at any page, but page 14 has been forced because every page shows page 14.

Next we see what I believe to be a beautifully disguised version of a simple trick called Magician's Choice. This is the name given to an effect where the magician gives an apparently free choice but the trick proceeds with whichever option the magician needs for the trick to work, rather than necessarily what was picked by the volunteer.

For an example, in a card trick a magician could place two piles of cards on the table and ask the volunteer to choose a pile. If the spectator chooses the pile on the left then the magician discards the other pile and the routine continues. But if the spectator chooses the pile on the right, then the magician asks the spectator to discard those cards, and picks up the pile on the left and the routine continues. The spectator sees the illusion of a free choice, but there was no choice at all.

In Derren's routine, I believe this same method is used extremely convincingly to force the audience spectator to choose page 14. Our volunteer tears the page down the middle leaving her with page 14 and another higher page number. Derren asks the spectator to hand one of the pages to either the lady on the left or the lady on the right. On the DVD, she hands page 14 to the lady to her left. This means Derren must ask the current volunteer to sit down and the lady to the left stands up and the routine continues. Had the volunteer kept page 14 for herself, the act would have continued with Derren confirming that our volunteer had discarded the other page, and the same lady would be standing up with page 14 instead of the lady to the left. All Derren is doing is looking at who has which page, and ensuring the show continues with the correct page in play. However simple this may sound, the trick is sold because Derren performs this so quickly, fluidly and phenomenally well.

The same "Magician's Choice" techniques are used in the next section. Derren knows what page 14 of the Daily Mail looks like, and he asks the new volunteer to pick one side of the newspaper as their "free" choice. However, it's the language he uses here that makes the difference. Once the volunteer is holding the page clearly in the air, having picked a page number herself, Derren asks, "what page number am I looking at?" and the volunteer says that he is looking at page 14. The volunteer is looking at the other side, page 13. So depending on the way she holds up the page, Derren could have asked "what page number are you looking at?" This is wonderful magic performance, and that's the second force of the evening taken care of. We have page 14 of the Daily Mail, and it's time to move on. The next thing to do is to ensure the word "influential" is chosen.

Melissa in the audience is instructed to tear up the page, and she makes a pile of torn newspapers. Derren allows

Melissa to make a free choice by handing whichever pile she chooses to Derren, discarding the other pile. This is genuinely a free choice, so this shows that the pile of papers that remains in play is not important. We can see that whilst the audience is clapping for Melissa as she returns to her seat, Derren is adding some newspapers to the pile. When the pile is placed on the table, it's clear that the top half of the papers are torn much smaller and more uniformly than those torn by Melissa. This appears to be because Derren has added his own pile of newspaper pieces to the torn pieces handed to him.

Derren sits at the table and asks Danni to pick a number between one and ten. This forces the chosen piece of paper to be one of the pieces that Derren placed onto the top of the pile. All these pieces of paper are surely identical, torn from multiple copies of the Daily Mail, page 14. There are a number of words on each piece but most of the words are very small and short. The only significant word on the piece is the word Influential. Danni chooses this word, and the trick is completed. Derren explains that there are other long words on the paper, and maybe there really was. Or maybe those words were printed over the torn edges and were not fully visible? Whatever the process, the random elements have been removed all the way through the trick. Derren reiterates that Danni could have changed her mind at many times, but in reality she doesn't, and wouldn't because there is no reason to.

Derren explains that it's genuinely a copy of that day's paper, and that's true – there's no reason why it couldn't be. However, when Derren returns to the stage to explain the whole process, the complexity of what he says adds a whole new level of mystery to the routine. Derren shows video footage from throughout the show and we can clearly see that he's been hiding secret messages in his performance. And if you own the DVD you can rewind and check, this is all true. He's been slipping references to the Daily Mail, page 14, "tear around influential" into the script all evening, and this convinces the audience that this is the real method to the performance. But it isn't. The real method is wonderful too of course, but Derren's explanation of subliminal messages and influencing the audience is a million times better and as the show ends, the audience leave the theatre utterly astonished at the extraordinary demonstration of mind control they just witnessed...

I've referred to this a number of times but it's always worth revisiting. As always, the secret is never the most impressive part of the routine. If you want to learn to be a magician, or if you are a magician who wants to learn to be better at being a magician, this is a beautiful, wonderful performance which takes a number of simple magic principles, presents them flawlessly and creates an illusion that is many times better than the trick should be. The straightforward methodology allows for a technically flawless performance that shouldn't go wrong, and the incredible showmanship gives the audience an experience that they will remember for years to come. They'll be stopping at the motorway services on the way home from the theatre to pick up a copy of the Daily Mail to check for the word on page 14. And it's there! Why wouldn't it be? What an incredible show this was.

An Evening of Wonders.

The Show.

Whilst Enigma is my favourite Derren Brown show, Evening of Wonders includes my favourite routine of all. The Oracle Act blew my mind when I first saw it performed live, so much so in fact that I went to see the show a second time to see if I could work out how it was done. I didn't actually work out a method until I saw the show a third time on DVD. When I watched the show for a fourth time to check my theory, I was amazed at how simple the method was. But we're getting ahead of ourselves. There's a wealth of great content in this show, and once again some of the simplest methods are dressed up into something much greater through outstanding performance. It's also another show that incorporates suggestion of a bigger effect going on. Words are flashed onto the back of the stage with the intention of making the audience believe that they are being influenced by the words used. I don't believe this myself and have a much simpler solution. Let's crack on, we have a lot to get through in this show.

Evening of Wonders starts with the claim that no actors or stooges are used in the show, and the audience's attention is drawn to a box which is hanging above the stage and will stay in clear view throughout the performance.

Setting up the Cash Gamble.

Derren's first trick is to offer an audience member a choice of two ice-creams – chocolate or tutti-frutti. He goes on to ask further questions, apparently to determine how the audience member chooses to answer multiple choice questions. The answers given are completely meaningless, but Derren makes out that he's using the answers given to determine which of two coloured boxes to bring onto the stage. Derren asks a stagehand to bring the green box to the stage, and then asks the audience member if they would like to guess how much money is in the box - £500 or £5000. If he guesses correctly then he gets to keep the money. The volunteer guesses £5000. Derren could show the box to contain £500 and the trick would be over, but as we discussed at the beginning of the book we need to focus on the performance and not the trick, so Derren allows the rest of the show for the volunteer to change his mind. There are trick boxes that you can buy from magic dealers that allow the magician to reveal whichever contents they choose. Derren appears to be using one of these boxes. Instead of a simple "what's in the box" game, he's concocted this elaborate rouse to suggest there are in fact two boxes and the one Derren brings on stage is chosen as a result of the psychological questioning earlier. In reality there's only one box and Derren could make the box show either cash amount at any time.

Setting up the banana trick.

Derren explains that at some point a man in a gorilla costume will come onto the stage and steal a banana from a table. In fact, this is a setup for a clever substitution trick later in the show. There's no need to keep your eye on the banana and miss the show.

20 Questions.

Derren randomly selects six audience members by throwing Frisbees into the audience. Each is given a number 1 – 6, although there's not really any need. When a magician does something that seems irrelevant and unnecessary you know there's probably a good reason. Then they are asked to write the name of an object on a piece of paper, on a table at the back of the stage. Derren goes over to the table and grabs a piece of paper with a 1 on it and sticks it on the front of the first volunteer. He then guesses that the first person thought of a rugby ball. Derren goes back to the table and grabs more numbers and sticks them on the other volunteers. There isn't any reason why these volunteers would need numbers on them, so we can only assume that these numbers are the key to the trick. We don't get to see close up what's on that table, but Derren appears to take a longer look at the pad when he's getting the numbers. This could be carbon paper, or a magic clipboard that transmits the image of the writing to a nearby screen. However he gets the information, Derren knows all six words, even though he pretends not to know what the volunteer named Holly has chosen. He knows of course, and this is a set-up for a nice reveal later. This is a great example of how Derren makes a trick bigger. Instead of revealing all six words, he pretends to miss one, only to throw it back out later in the show. Derren asks questions to the final volunteer, instructing them to answer silently in their head. This is all misdirection because we know Derren already knows the word, and again he's making something much bigger out of a very simple illusion.

After revisiting the banana, Dan's box of money and other setups, we move onto the next routine.

Telephone Prediction.

Derren takes one volunteer for the next trick, and they set up a telephone conversation. Derren asks a number of questions for a bit of insider knowledge about the person they are going to call. Derren knows his name, occupation, hobbies and pet names. Derren explains that at the end of the call he will ask the caller to say a 3 digit number, and he predicts that the number will be 347.

The caller guesses a three digit number but it's way off. 116 followed by a second guess of 529 – nowhere near. But of course, this isn't the actual trick; this is the setup for a prediction. Derren offered a £10 prize, and at the end of the trick these numbers will be the numbers on the banknote. So how does he make this happen? You have to look really closely at this one but there seems to be a substitution when the note comes out of Derren's pocket. Being honest, I don't know specifically how the note is printed, but there's a lot of time to get the note made up. The numbers are chosen at 21m 38s on the DVD, and note is given to the volunteer at 24m 18s, nearly three minutes later. Could this be produced by a pocket sized printer? You can see when he reaches for the pocket that the note is switched. I keep looking at that mobile phone and have to admit I've never seen a mobile that looks like this one. Is it a prop? Whatever the method, the numbers are printed (or maybe the entire note is printed) after the numbers are spoken on stage.

Money Box Reveal.

Derren simply removes the cover from the box to reveal the appropriate amount needed. A very clever trick box, you can see there is an optical illusion design where the bottom section of the box (complete with small feet, gold band and brown stripe) leaves a large section of this apparently empty box hidden. This is where the other cash amount slips down into so it can't be seen. The performer simply removes the cover in one of two ways, one revealing the smaller cash amount and the other the larger.

Gorilla Switcher.

As Derren walks to the left of the stage to pick up the whiteboard he slips behind the wings and a double picks up the whiteboard and carries it to the other side of the stage. Derren slips into the gorilla costume with help from a stagehand no doubt. I believe this costume has no back at all, and can easily be slipped onto the front of his suit whilst the audience believes that Derren is still on stage, carrying the whiteboard.

Interval.

Derren instructs audience members to take a card and envelope from the stewards waiting around the auditorium during the interval. He explains that there is space to write a question on the card, and we are instructed to write our seat location and row with our initials on the outside of the black envelope (for example JB, Dress Circle, Row A). Stewards guard the stage and audience members are allowed up one at a time to put the cards in their sealed envelopes into a glass bowl. By the end of the break there are at least a hundred cards in the bowl, but this distracts us from a very important point that appears so simple that we overlook it. The bowl has been in view since before the show started and there were already cards in it as we were taking our seats. A small throwaway comment from Derren advises us that some of the audience have filled in cards already on the way into the venue, but for anyone else that would like to take part, they can do so during the interval. This small point masks a much bigger secret. As the audience thinks of questions to ask Derren, they write on the cards, seal them in the black envelopes and head down to the stage to place them in the bowl. The bowl stays in view and no-one tampers with these cards, which will be used by Derren during the Oracle act in the second half. Anyone in the audience who fills in one of these cards now knows that the cards are printed, "Your Question", and that's all they have written inside – one question for Derren, and nothing else. It's important that as many people as possible fill in these cards, because if the audience has seen the cards with their own eyes, they will know that there was only space to write your question for Derren. This is a great convincer, and we'll see why when the Oracle act takes place.

Ideomotor Phenomenon and Table Turning.

Members of the audience are needed for a demonstration of table-turning. Derren needs volunteers that are susceptible to believe what's about to happen and will simply go along with it, and a demonstration of the Ideomotor Phenomenon is a great way to do this. Each volunteer is given a chain with a heavy nut attached to the end. They hold this at arm's length and Derren suggests that it will start to move on its own. This is a scientific phenomenon, discovered in the 1800s where the subject makes tiny motions unconsciously with their hand and the outstretched arm. These movements are amplified by the length of the chain, causing much larger movement in the swinging bolt. This phenomenon is often attributed to explanations of water dowsing, Ouija Boards and so on.

This leads into a demonstration of Table Turning, where Derren introduces a "name box", which is a definite load of hokum – the name box is part of the floating table effect that follows. By introducing the name box at this stage it takes the focus away from the mechanics of the floating table effect to follow.

Table turning is another classic effect that simply just works. It helps to have a table that is easy to move and I would suggest that the one used on the show is likely to have castors or something smooth at the feet to allow the table to be slid around. By asking a group of people to lay their hands on the table and willing them to allow the table to move freely it only takes one of the volunteers to make a small involuntary movement and the table will start to shift. As everyone else involved allows this to happen they will subconsciously push the table in the same direction. The large movement of the table distracts the volunteers from the tiny contribution they are making, and they each believe they are not responsible for the movement. This is a great demonstration of the Ideomotor Phenomenon, and performing it using volunteers who already showed their susceptibility to the effect in the earlier trick is a brilliant piece of magical thinking.

Floating Table.

The floating table effect is a beautiful piece of magic, created by German magician, Dirk Losander. Losander's magic is famous among magicians for its artistry and beauty. Many magic dealers sell floating tables, but Losander makes the best ones. They look heavy and solid but in reality are extremely light and easy to float. To create a convincing effect takes a great deal of practice and I've seen magicians performing this routine without any of the subtlety and magic of Losander. Derren Brown's performance here is the closest I have seen to Losander's famous routine.

The floating table is often made from balsa wood, and weighs practically nothing. The table is painted to look like a heavy wooden table and a tablecloth is draped over the top. The cloth is attached to the surface of the table, usually with magnets. A wire runs from one corner of the tablecloth to the table itself and the magician can make small movements of the end of the wire they are holding, resulting in larger movements of the table. You can see that whilst the audience volunteer moves his hands occasionally, Derren is always holding the tablecloth in one hand. The other hand can let go of the table if needed as the controlling hand is always in place, holding the corner of the table cloth and the end of the wire, moving the table as needed.

So, what about the name box we saw earlier? Losander tables come with the box as standard. The box is also painted to look like a wooden box but the base is magnetic. This is used as a brilliant convincer because it allows the magician to hold the table by the box instead of the tablecloth. You can see that Derren looks inside the name box by cleverly keeping hold of the table whilst looking like he is letting go. The right hand manipulates the wire allowing the magician to lift the table. Derren then takes hold of the name box in his left hand. This allows him to let go of the tablecloth and open the box with his right hand, then reach back for the tablecloth before letting go of the box. The beauty of this routine lies with the timing. Just as the audience might start to think that Derren is manipulating the table somehow, he appears to let go completely and look inside the name box. In fact, the name box is attached to the surface of the table by magnets, and there's always a hand on either the box or the cloth, so the table is always suspended.

Another great touch is when the table seems to be floating unaided and Derren puts one hand on the surface of the table to push it back down. Magicians use something called a PK Ring which looks like a piece of jewellery and is worn on the finger like any other ring. These rings contain powerful magnets, so by wearing one and placing a flat hand on the table surface the magician can easily push down to appear to be preventing the table from floating, or move their hand higher to suggest the table is full of helium and is trying to get away. Again, the theory is quite straightforward, but the presentation is anything but. If you want a frame of reference to know how well Derren performs this trick, there are many videos on YouTube of magicians floating tables badly, or using cheaply made imitation versions of Losander's famous prop. I've yet to see any performance that is more impressive than Derren or Dirk's presentation.

Oracle Act.

During the interval, audience members were allowed onto the stage one at a time to put their envelopes in a glass bowl, and their cards, sealed inside, now contain a question for Derren to answer. Derren takes a card from the bowl, and reads the initials and seat number from the outside of the sealed envelope. This leads us to the first audience member, Katie. As far as the audience is concerned, Katie has filled out her card with a question, placed it in the bowl during the interval and now it's been picked out at random. But I disagree. Let's look in more detail at the order of events that lead to Katie filling out her question on her card.

Remember the glass bowl had some cards in before the interval? Earlier, Derren briefly mentioned that some people had filled in their card on the way into the venue, and these cards were the ones that were already in view in the glass bowl. That's not what I think. I believe the cards that were filled out by the audience volunteers on the way into the theatre never made it into the bowl, and were taken backstage to be examined by the crew.

The cards we see in the bowl are just dummy envelopes and these can be ignored. The audience spent their time during the interval filling in a question on their cards, sealing them in the envelopes and dropping them in the bowl on top of the dummy cards. These cards may be used as props in the performance, but none of the content will be used, because how could that be possible? The envelopes are opaque and we can see that no-one has tampered with the cards or the bowl. If you filled in a card during the interval, then I'm sorry but there is no way it would be used in the show – the preparation for this act is being carried out during the first half of the performance, backstage, using the cards that were filled out by audience members before the show started.

The backstage team have decided that Katie's card is a good one, based on the information she filled in **before the show, as she entered the theatre**. On stage, the cards from the bowl are reduced to mere props and the card in Derren's hand could be any of the cards from the bowl. As Derren looks at the envelope he's pretending to read the details from it whilst reciting the information he memorised from Katie's card backstage during the interval.

Here we see a great example of pre-show work, and dual reality combined. The audience think they know exactly what is going on, because a false reality has been planted in their memory. They have seen the cards and envelopes with their own eyes, queued up to place their own in the bowl, and seen that everything appears normal. The bowl has not been tampered with and the cards remain in view all the way through the interval. But, when Katie wrote on her card before the show began, she filled in much more information than we realise. Instead of writing only a question, she filled in her name, her date of birth, something Derren could not possibly know and a question you would like to ask Derren. If you listen carefully to the conversation, all Derren knows for certain is that the girls name is Katie, she is 19 years old, she changed her hair colour that same day, and wants to know if she will travel to America. Derren adds a couple of cold reading statements that would apply to any 19 year old girl, and makes an excellent job of giving the impression that he is revealing a great deal of information. The reality is he only has the information from the card.

But hold on a moment – we've seen these cards ourselves and even filled them out and dropped them in the bowl. Printed on the card was, "Your Question". There were no spaces to fill in date of birth, or any of the other information. Why would Katie have written down that she changed her hair colour? Why did she give her date of birth or any other information?

This is the genius of the routine. You, the audience member, saw the cards and therefore you know that Derren could not possibly know any of the information he revealed. **But you didn't see the cards that were being filled in earlier in the foyer before the show started.** Those cards could indeed have spaces clearly marked for the volunteers to fill out all the things that Katie wrote and any other information Derren could use. The beauty of this routine is that the cards filled out in the foyer are the only ones being read out during the act and those cards are different to the ones that the remaining 99% of the audience have seen.

Now we know the layout of the information on the earlier set of cards, we can see how this works with the other volunteers, but first, a distraction.

The next envelope Derren takes from the bowl is written in scruffy handwriting, and Derren uses his psychic powers to determine that this card was probably written by a teenage boy, out to impress his friends, and it probably just says "Why are you a wanker?" or something. This card is thrown away into the audience because it's not going to be suitable for the trick. Someone in the crowd actually picks up the envelope and reads the card. It simply says "cock!" Later in the show, Derren remarks, "That kid was right, I am a cock!" as a call-back to that moment. But how did Derren know this was a rude card from just the handwriting? The reality is simple. Derren slipped this envelope into the pile himself. This happens in every show, and Derren can confidently throw the card away towards the audience, safe in the knowledge that someone is bound to pick it up and open it. Again, this is a brilliant convincer that he's using some sort of psychic ability because this random unexpected rude card seems completely off script to an unsuspecting audience.

Back on topic, Derren takes another card from the bowl and pretends to read the outside of the envelope, whilst reciting from memory the details from the second of his pre-show cards. He acts the part brilliantly, sounding like he is fishing for clues, clutching at threads and revealing information a piece at a time. But we know the format of the information on those pre-show cards, and listening carefully reveals the same format every time.

Someone with the initials CKO is 35 years old, bought a dress from EBay and wants to buy a cat.

Someone called "Sashan" is from Uganda, and is going on holiday to Iceland on his own.

Another incredibly convincing part of the act follows as Derren shifts the tone of the show and moves onto the next stage of the Oracle Act. Derren blindfolds himself and moves away from the envelopes and the cards, and asks members of the audience to mentally transmit thoughts to him. The reality is Derren is presenting the same Oracle Act, but by explaining that he's no longer using the cards the audience think he's moved on to something different. He's still using the information that was written on the cards of course, but the audience's attention is drawn away from this by the shift in tone, and the presentation tells the audience that he's now moving into direct mind reading of any audience members. They forget about the bowl and the cards and Derren moves their attention to the next section of this routine. Whilst the presentation is very different, the method remains the same.

Instead of telling the volunteers their age, he tells them their star sign. This is certainly possible if you know the birth date but by delivering the same information in a different way this further separates this section of the act from the previous part. Derren says he is receiving the thoughts from someone with Initials AW in the stalls. This information was also from a card memorised earlier, and he reveals that AW won their house in a competition.

The rest of the Oracle Act gets faster and more intense as Derren appears to be on the verge of collapse. Throughout this section, it's worth noting that only 4 people have been spoken to. Your memory of the show after the event plays tricks and it always feels like many more people were involved. The last volunteer (Kelly) starts to be bombarded with information, and as Derren gets more vague he starts to ramble about security and front doors. He asks for a glass of water that never comes. He rambles further on a number of topics, suggesting he knows an awful lot about Kelly, but in this faster and faster delivery Kelly is never given the chance to confirm or deny the accuracy of any of what has been said. We know Kelly's star sign; she runs a bookshop and lost her Dad recently. She has a Cat. Everything else is fluff and presentation, until with a crash Derren falls to the floor and the curtains are closed.

The Oracle Act is one of the best pieces of magic performance I have ever seen.

The Hanging Box.

At the end of the show, Derren remembers the hanging box. It's been in full view of the audience from the beginning of the show. Derren explains that before the audience arrives, he sits in the theatre on his own and tries to imagine what will happen throughout the show that night. He writes this out, puts it in the box and this prediction hangs there throughout the show. This is clearly impossible and the information must be written during the show as the events are happening. But if that's the method, how do they get the completed prediction paper in the box? And specifically how does he get this information right up to events that happen only moments earlier? The prediction contains information about the volunteer Danielle, she's picked at random from the audience and the box is opened with the prediction written out in full within the space of a minute. How can that possibly happen?

Danielle, the volunteer that helps with the trick is selected from the audience at 1h 06m on the DVD. I suggest that she was chosen to participate by the show much earlier, without her knowledge.

Throughout the show, a stagehand is writing the prediction as the events occur. Danielle's details are added to the roll before she's even on the stage, or been picked. The details on the prediction describe her gender, hair, clothing, all things you can see just by looking. The only information in the prediction that couldn't be written out in advance is that Danielle's number guess would be off by three. We'll consider how this works when we look at how Danielle was chosen.

So now we know that the prediction is already written out in full with all the specifics of the show, including Danielle's details. She's sat in the audience, completely unaware that she has already been chosen by the crew to be a participant in the show later, and all her details are already written out. All that remains to be done is to get the prediction on stage and into the box, then randomly pick a volunteer in a way that looks like free choice but guarantees that Danielle is chosen.

Derren explains that he will choose a psychic volunteer for the big reveal. Derren, apparently completely randomly chooses three people from the audience, one of which is Danielle. He asks each of them to guess a number that he wrote on a piece of card in his hand. In reality, he only pretended to write a number, and the card remains blank as it goes into the envelope. He specifies that each of the three volunteers must choose a number that is no-where near other chosen numbers. The reason for this is because unknown to Danielle, when she chooses a number Derren is simply going to use his nail to write a number that is off by three on the card in his hand. A sheet of carbon paper in the envelope makes the scratch of the nail on the envelope turn into writing on the card inside. In other words regardless of what numbers were said, Derren was always going to pick Danielle and the number he writes was always going to be off by three. This is vital because the prediction is already on the stage at this point with all Danielle's details written down. The box is still hanging up but the prediction roll was completed before Danielle even made it onto the stage. So where is it?

 The box is lowered onto a table. You can see that as Derren takes the key to open the padlock of the box, he reaches down to the underside of the table and lifts something into the front of the box. The box Derren is using looks exactly like the Malloy Magic Master Prediction System, which can be viewed on the website of the manufacturer. Purchase of this box also includes a table, and there are versions of this trick that come with different tables at different price points. Therefore we know that the table is part of the routine – there are no options to buy the box without a table and I suspect the trick would not be possible if the performer only had the box and a regular table. The completed prediction is hidden within the table, the box is lowered onto it and during the unlocking process the tube with the prediction inside is taken from the table into the box.

This is why the trick is so wonderful and convincing. The prediction contains information from points throughout the show, but even contains the prediction that Danielle's guess would be off by three, and information on what she was wearing. All this had to be predicted before she came onto the stage. It really was – because they chose the volunteer much earlier in the show than she thinks they did. It's genius.

Enigma.

The show.

As always, if you have not seen the show, stop reading and get the DVD. This show is absolutely incredible, and to look into the methods without first experiencing it as it should be seen would be a crime! This is my favourite show overall, and I don't think I will ever see a theatrical presentation where the audience reaction is as strong as this - so many standing ovations in one show! The buzz of the crowd as they left. Enigma is a truly wonderful two hours and this is the standard every working magician in the world should be aiming for.

Introduction.

During the opening speech, before the show starts, Derren does sneak a cheeky reference to the band McFly as he asks 'Perhaps there's a holiday destination you'd like to McFly to?' This is one of the things I love about his presentation, it's nothing to do with any method, but some people will hear it and wonder if there's some subliminal programming going on.

And so the show begins. A basket is placed onto the stage, and up to 60 audience members are invited to write their three favourite things on a slip of paper and pop it in the basket. There are only 60 pieces of paper, but it won't matter what people write because the basket is modified to allow the performer to switch the audience papers with 60 identical papers. You can see from the DVD that the basket has a cloth interior, and underneath this cloth there are 60 identical pieces of paper, written by Derren's team with the same three words written on each. The audience put their slips of paper in the basket, but the special compartments are switched before the one slip of paper is removed. It won't matter which paper is picked because they all have the same three words written on - McFly, Cookie and Cider.

Derren will pretend to have never heard of McFly shortly.

First a game of "word disassociation" is played. This adds to the presentation significantly. Derren convinces the audience that the random words being suggested by the volunteer have some relevance to the word 'cookie' that Derren will guess shortly. But we know the slips of paper all said 'cookie' and also all said 'McFly" and 'cider' as well. Later in the show, Derren stops what he's saying very suddenly, then hurries to the whiteboard to predict the remaining word on the paper. This word is cider, and Derren's prediction turns out to be the page number in the dictionary that Derren handed out earlier. This is just a wonderful bit of extra presentation which adds further ambiguity to the method and the overall routine. The page number in the dictionary will be the same every show, because the word being guessed is the same word every night.

Derren hands out a brown envelope to an audience member to keep safe. This envelope contains a prediction regarding a picture of confetti. There's no trick here, but it will just be revealed near the end of the show as part of a stunning finale.

Guess Whom.

A number of photographs of audience members are shown. These photos were apparently taken in the foyer before the show. On the DVD, we can see some of the audience members watching the show. However, I believe that the five or so people seen are the only ones in the deck, and the rest of the cards are the same every show. This is a great example of presentation over content. Imagine this trick performed with a regular marked deck of cards. Each of the spectators takes one of the cards from the deck. Derren can glimpse which cards were selected by each of the volunteers by looking at the secret mark on the back of the card when it is re-inserted into the pack. The way that Derren asks the spectator to return the card to the pack (Derren dribbles the cards from one hand to the other) provides ample time to see which card was selected by each volunteer. I'd also suggest that this pack of photographs is the same every show, as Derren asks the audience not to be 'disappointed if we didn't use your photo, it's nothing personal, we just can't use them all'. It would be a lot of work to make a customised marked deck from audience photographs every night, and this one line of dialogue makes everyone in the audience believe that Derren used other people's photos. In fact, only five photos were used. The rest of the performance is simply a great presentation of "was that your card?"

The final part of this routine involves having the five or so people stand up in the audience, and the last person standing is the final predicted, forced card.

The Box.

Another fantastic example of doing an incredible illusion in a way that cannot fail is The Box. All you need to know about this trick is that the audience volunteer reveals the name of her grandmother at 16 minutes 50 seconds on the DVD. This is before she's even started to head to the stage. It is important that the name is revealed as soon as possible for this trick, because the end result features an engraved coin found in an impossible location, so the backstage team need to get that coin engraved quickly.

Derren tells a "true" story that happened over two years after his grandfather died. Derren tells this story beautifully, and it's almost a shame that the story is almost certainly not true. If the story is true, it's a strange coincidence that it mirrors an existing magic illusion that can be bought from magic dealers. After Derren tells the beginning of the story, he breaks off to ask the volunteer onto the stage. I believe that Derren receives a signal from the backstage crew that alerts him that the engraving machine has been set up with the correct name. It makes sense to get the volunteer on stage at this point so that the audience applause would drown out the sound of the engraving.

The engraved coin is sneaked onto the stage when Derren walks to the right to get the microphone. The method for getting the coin inside the box and the ball of wool is not something I can reveal here, but if you wished to type into Google words such as "Nested Boxes Magic Trick", or "coin into ball of wool magic trick", you will able to locate magic dealers that will be happy to sell you a complete kit!

Interval.

Audience members are invited to go up on stage during the interval to choose a picture at random by placing a cross on the pad next to the image of their choice. Confetti is ultimately revealed to be the most popular option, but as this has to be the case to allow the finale effect to work, the crosses left by the audience do not matter as the pad will be switched before the votes are counted.

Somnambulism.

This is a really great demonstration of hypnosis, and there isn't room in this book to explain how hypnosis works. However, in an audience some 2000 strong, the temptation for some people to just play along is overwhelming. The language that Derren uses is very persuasive, as he describes at the beginning of the piece that people who respond to this are those with the most 'natural talent'. All the way through, Derren's words encourage participation. The knowledge that joining in may mean that Derren chooses you to go on stage for the next section is enough to get people to play along. Having said all that, there is also a definite case for hypnosis being real, and I am sure that Derren Brown is an expert in the subject, and the way this plays out in a large theatre means that only a small percentage of people need to be susceptible to the suggestion in order for it to have a great effect for everyone, whether watching or joining in.

Spirit Cabinet.

The Spirit Cabinet is a wonderful piece of chorography, which definitely should be viewed before reading the method and once again after. The presentation convinces you that you have seen things that prevent the method from working. For example, how could someone secretly enter the cabinet when people were watching from both sides? The solution is astonishing.

As the cabinet is brought onto the stage, a stagehand sneaks behind it under cover of the shadows. He can reach inside the cabinet to ring the bell. The curtain is whipped back open quickly in order to make the whole cabinet move, covering up any remaining movement of the back curtain.

The ball in the glass is achieved by using a sponge ball, which is in the pocket of the stagehand, squeezed into a small tube. When the curtain is drawn the stagehand puts the tube between the volunteer's fingers, and pushes the sponge ball out. This expands as it lands in the bottom of the glass.

The first example of spirit writing is completed in the same way, with the stagehand writing in chalk on the slate. The second demonstration works in a different way. One of the two new slates has an extra slate piece that fits perfectly into the wooden frame. The second slate has a letter O written on, and the loose piece of slate has a J on. The two slates are placed with the written sides face to face, giving the appearance of only one slate with no writing. When Derren shows the two blank slates you can see how he is holding the loose piece of slate in the frame with the tips of his fingers. When he gives the two slates to the volunteer, they are held tightly together and turned over. The loose piece of slate falls into the frame of the first slate, so when they are opened up one slate appears to have the J written on, and the other actually does have the O written on it.

In the next section of this routine, the spectator suddenly jumps up out of the chair. This is a gimmicked electric chair.

Finally, all three volunteers are placed into the spirit cabinet. The stagehand goes wild, throwing paper out of the top, shouting and shaking the box before jumping out of the back of the box.

The stage management of this whole routine is exceptional, with spectators looking around all the sides of the box at the correct times so they will not see the stagehand. Derren asks the spectators to go and check something then 'come back and stand there just where you are now.' Everything is choreographed perfectly to give the illusion that the spectators are guarding the box from all directions, where in reality they only see the back of the box when the stagehand is inside, and so on. Also, when the routine is over, the cabinet's curtains are rolled back completely, but there is enough room for the stagehand to stand upright in the columns of material.

Finale – The Enigma Code.

The crucial point in figuring out the finale of Enigma is knowing that the show must end with the pictures in a fixed order, whilst Derren spends almost the entire finale talking about generating random numbers. Derren explains that "nothing is random", and in this finale it's true – nothing is actually random. The finale revisits the pictures that were displayed during the interval. These pictures are confetti, an egg, a needle, ice-cream, a goose, a moose and a glass of apple juice. Having seen the show, you know now that the initials of these items spell the word Enigma, as long as you ignore the confetti. During the interval, the audience was invited to go onto the stage and put a cross next to one image they would like to choose at random, and at the beginning of the finale a member of the audience is given the pad to total up which was the most popular image. However, this would be random, and as Derren says, "nothing is random!" The pad is on stage throughout the interval, and at the end of the interval, the pad is switched (perhaps even as simply as turning it over to reveal prepared pages from the back of the pad). The columns that are added up by the audience member are not the votes placed by the audience, but a pre-prepared page which lists confetti as the most popular choice.

Next, six male volunteers are invited on stage, and they have a number attached to their chests as they arrive. They are asked to stand in a random order in front of lollipop signs marked A to F. In order to make this completely random, Derren asks the group to move into a 'New Order' (complete with Blue Monday music playing!). The random number generated is 132645, and this is the only truly random element to this show. Behind the scenes, a stagehand has six copies of each image from the interval numbered one to six. He has six eggs, six needles, six geese, six mooses (meese?), and six apple juices. Our volunteers are already standing in the random order they chose, and we know the images need to spell out Enigma. Therefore our stagehand needs to choose the Egg picture with the number 1, the Needle with number 3, Ice Cream 2, Goose 6, Moose 4, and Apple Juice 5.

Another volunteer comes onto the stage, and is asked to choose one of the letters, she chooses C, and she shakes hands with the man standing in position C. This handshake and the ongoing discussion of making a psychic connection allows time for the stagehand to put this new prediction (C) into another envelope. For this, he only needs to choose one of six images. These are A – egg, B – Needle, C - Ice Cream, D – Goose, E – Moose, F – Apple juice. There's no need to have 6 of each image for this prediction because the images will always spell Enigma so only one image for each letter is needed. The envelopes are held together with an elastic band and placed at the back of the stage whilst the distraction of the handshake goes on.

Derren asks the last volunteer to take the envelopes from the back of the stage. The first image at the top of the pile is the C prediction, which is placed at the front of the stage. An envelope containing a set of all the pictures is passed to the female volunteer The other envelope contains the Enigma images numbered correctly to match the order of the people on stage.

Derren returns to the female volunteer and performs a card force. This is a psychological force that can be learned in full on Derren's 'The Devil's Picturebook' DVD set. He only has six cards in his hands and he begins to deal them onto the table one at a time, whilst explaining that he wants the volunteer to say 'stop' at any time they like. This is a very clever card force, which relies on the volunteer not knowing what they are supposed to be doing until about half of the cards are already dealt. Once Derren has explained what to do, the spectator can see there are not many cards left. Derren can also deal the cards slowly and when the spectator says stop the card will be either just dealt, being dealt, or next to be dealt. Derren knows that the order of pictures is not random, so he can use this method to force the ice cream card because the spectator said C, and Ice Cream will always be in the third position because it represents the third letter of ENIGMA. To see a clearer demonstration of this card force, check out the card routine on the DVD extras of the Evening of Wonders DVD.

The next section contains more presentation and performance, including the reveal that the card at the front of the stage also shows C and Ice Cream. This is also not random as covered earlier in this book. These envelopes were all brought onto the stage after the decision was made by the volunteer.

The next reveal involves the audience member who has totalled up the crosses on the pad from the interval to find (surprise surprise) that the Confetti image was the most popular choice. We know that this has been rigged, but to the audience this is another coincidence – Confetti is missing from the display on stage! It's also in the envelope that was handed to the audience member at the start of the show. Derren continues to explain that nothing is random, and he's right because the pad was switched to show a page where the confetti column had received the most votes, regardless of what the audience actually chose. The method is so simple, and yet we are distracted by the prediction envelopes and now the reveal that the two decorative columns at the side of the stage have a hidden "Choose the Confetti" message when rolled together.

Finally, the reveal that Derren really did know who McFly were, as a music video plays and of course the song lyrics match the display on stage – The first reveal is that 'the order will be an egg and a needle and then an ice cream – goose and moose and apple juice oh yeah!'. The second reveal hits the audience as if an even better trick has taken place, as the lollypop sticks are rotated to show the matching images. But they would match, wouldn't they? Because as the final reveal shows us, as the audience starts on their third standing ovation, the initials of the images spells out Enigma, the name of the best live show I ever saw.

Svengali.

Svengali continues in a similar vein to previous shows, favouring magic, showmanship, illusion and psychology over the circus skills and feats of endurance seen in Something Wicked This Way Comes. The highlight of this show is the Svengali itself, an automaton doll that performs mind reading effects similar to those that Derren himself usually carries out. Is the story of the Svengali doll everything it appears? Probably not. The word Svengali can refer to many things associated with magic performance. There is a Svengali deck of cards which allow many wonderful card tricks to be performed with little to no skill from the magician. Svengali is also a fictional character in the novel, Trilby, and Wikipedia says that the word itself has come to refer to a person who, with evil intent, **dominates, manipulates and controls a creative person such as an actor**. Could the name Svengali have been chosen by Derren as a sly wink to the magicians who recognise the name as a well known magical prop? Or could it be that this automaton is being manipulated and controlled by a creative person (such as an actor)? Or is the story he tells about the Svengali Doll completely true? Was this doll based on the death mask of a six year old Hungarian? Did this doll really get auctioned in secret, only to end up in Derren's live show? A quick Google of words like "Svengali Hungary Doll" gives many search results, with almost all of them being discussion of this show, and very few references to the actual story Derren refers to. Perhaps we will never find the truth about the Svengali. Or perhaps the automaton doll we see is being controlled and manipulated by a creative person off-stage. We'll never know.

Where is Derren's Shoe?

As always, wonderful presentation serves to distract from the simplicity of the trick. Derren arrives on stage only wearing one shoe. The audience volunteers are selected to play a game of "Find the Shoe". On the stage are three tables, each with a cardboard shoe box on. Ostensibly one of these boxes contains Derren's shoe and it's up to the audience to guess which box the shoe is in.

As mentioned, I love the presentation of this effect. Derren uses psychology and showmanship, combined with plenty of witty banter, to make sure that the audience volunteers never guess which box his shoe is in. The key to this trick is not the psychology he explains, but in the boxes themselves.

It's impossible for me to reveal the exact method that is being used, but I can explain ways in which it could be done. There's simply no way that Derren can be sure which box the audience member will choose, so he needs to have all options covered. He needs to be able to open each of the three boxes and to show the box is empty, or full, as the routine requires. Let's say that the audience member chooses box two. This means that Derren needs to open this box and show it is empty. If the audience member chose boxes one and three, then Derren will need to open box two to reveal the shoe. We need to ignore all the presentation and performance and concentrate on the boxes. How can Derren open the box to show it's empty or full as needed?

My methods for this routine involve gimmicked boxes. My most likely theory is based on the checkerboard pattern printed inside the boxes. Imagine a shoebox like those used on stage. There are four walls and a base to the main box, and a lid that slots on top. If I was performing this trick, I'd have a mirror in the box, at a 45 degree angle running across the diagonal of the sides of the box from front to back. The shoe could be stored behind this mirror. In this situation the box lid can be removed, and when the observer looks inside they see an apparently empty box. In fact, the audience is seeing the bottom half of the box reflected in the top half. My expectation is that this is how Derren performs the routine as the checkerboard pattern inside the box provides the cover for the mirror running along the diagonal length of the box sides.

The back panel of the box also could hold a secret, being hinged and attached to the mirror. Behind the mirror is another back panel for the box, which is hidden by the mirror which also hides the shoe. When Derren needs to reveal the box containing the shoe, he pushes the invisible back panel into place, the mirror rotates and faces the floor, and the shoe can be seen. In my version of this effect the back panel and the mirror rotate as one unit, so as the shoe is pushed into visibility the mirror becomes the floor of the box. In a large theatrical production such as this there is also the opportunity to invest in extra props, and it would surprise me to see if there was a trapdoor in the surface of the table, or other gimmicks to allow the empty box to be shown completely empty by ditching the shoe if not needed.

Secret Confessions.

Derren chooses a seat number at random (in the TV broadcast of this show the seat was J7). Derren has asked audience members to write a secret confession, and Derren has a glass bowl with many slips of paper with confessions on. Theatre staff and ushers were handing out slips of paper as audience members made their way into the theatre. No-one in the audience is an actor or a stooge.

Derren uses a tombola drum to choose a seat number. It's clearly visible that there are 1499 plastic discs in the tombola, and we can see different seat numbers printed on the disks. Magic dealers often sell innocent looking props that are cleverly gimmicked for magicians, and I am aware of the magic tombola. These look ordinary enough but have different sections inside the drum. The magician puts their hand inside to choose a disc but their hand goes into a smaller compartment made of transparent plastic. In this compartment all the disks could have the same seat number on. Multiple coloured disks can be used and the magician can pull out a handful and throw some back in the drum. This further sells the illusion that any seat number could have been picked from the tombola. So we now know that whichever disc is chosen from the tombola, the seat number "randomly" chosen will be J7, or whatever seat Derren wishes to use that night.

All that's required now is for the ushers and theatre staff to keep note of the confession that will be used in the act. Let's assume that the usher hands out pieces of paper which are pre-printed with spaces for name, seat number, and confession. Before the show, the team can look through the confessions, find a good one, put the seat number onto a handful of plastic discs and load them into the separate compartment. During the show, Derren chooses the disk and random, and reads out the confession.

Psychic Painting.

Probably the best demonstration of performance over method of all the live shows, Derren paints a portrait of a celebrity by reading the thoughts of an audience volunteer. The volunteer is asked to picture the celebrity in their mind, as if it was on a large screen with bright colours and vivid imagery. This is a wonderful routine which is so incredibly simple it almost defies belief. Derren's obvious portrait painting skills are demonstrated and the performance definitely suggests that mind reading is involved. However as I'm sure you will have guessed by now there is no mind reading going on. In my method, the process is not taking place during the painting, but during the set-up of the trick. All that Derren needs to know is the name of the celebrity he needs to draw. What would happen for example, if the chosen celebrity was someone Derren had never heard of? How would he draw someone if he didn't know what they looked like?

The solution is to force the celebrity choice to ensure that Derren will know who it is before the trick even starts. And the secret lies in the net. You remember the net, right? It was used to collect the audience suggestions, then passed to the volunteer to choose one. Like the tombola earlier, this net is not what it appears to be. This is an innocent looking version of what magicians call the "change bag". The bag (or in this case, the net) has two compartments. Before the routine begins, one compartment is empty, and the other contains a handful of papers, each one folded into four, and each one with the name Elvis Presley. Then the compartment is switched, often by way of a mechanism built into the handle. This leaves an ordinary looking empty net. During the routine, various audience members write the names of any celebrity they choose on their papers, fold them up and put them in the net. When all the names have been collected the net is raised, swung around to the volunteer about to go on stage, the mechanism is switched and the volunteer chooses a name at random from the net. This looks like he's choosing one of the slips of paper written by the audience, but every slip in this compartment has the same name on. When the painting is drawn, each of the audience volunteers assumes that the celebrity was chosen by one of the others. In fact, no-one in the audience wrote that name, and Derren could paint Elvis on every night of the theatrical run if he wanted to!

Last confession, sealed in envelope.

This routine is pretty much the same as the tombola routine we saw earlier. The confession that was randomly picked from the bowl earlier and sealed in the envelope was indeed random. Magicians can easily make envelopes that open and seal at both ends. When Derren's team were setting up the tombola trick earlier, they could choose another confession and seal this in one compartment of the envelope. When the random paper is sealed in the envelope during the show, it goes in the other compartment and stays there. Derren comes back to the envelope for this part of the show, and the envelope is opened at the other end. The audience volunteer removes the paper slip with the confession which was placed there earlier in the evening, and not the one that was picked during the performance. Derren knows the seat number, just as he did in the tombola routine earlier. The selection of the audience member using a torch is lovely presentation as he eliminates the audience members one at a time. But Derren knows all along which spectator to choose and he uses great acting skills to make it appear that he is eliminating the other audience members for reasons of the way they stand, speak and so on.

Svengali.

After another demonstration of hypnosis, convincing the audience that their fingers are stuck together, Derren gets a volunteer onto the stage and we are introduced to the doll, Svengali.

The Svengali doll is apparently a clockwork automaton and Derren is seen to be winding it up before the performance. The first demonstration is that the Svengali doll responds to the sound of a bell. Working on the basis that the Svengali doll story is a work of fiction, I believe it is safe to assume this doll has been built by Derren's team for this performance.

The next part of the demonstration went on a lot longer when I saw this show live and his been chopped down for the television broadcast. The apparent hypnosis means the audiences hands stick together like glue. In the live performance Derren convinces the audience that their fingers are stuck together before the part you see on the broadcast version. The overall sequence is a combination of the audience willing the process to work, muscle memory (where if you hold your hand in the position he instructs it does start to feel like your fingers are sticking together) and the use of language ("Just let it happen" and other positive phrases designed to make the audience members want to join in). The whole performance including the selection of the volunteer is classic suggestion and showmanship. It's so easy for the audience to watch the spectator's arm rising and falling on command and wondering what is going on to make it happen. But in reality it's stage hypnosis, suggestion and simply joining in and playing along.

The next section is a great example of dual reality and clever use of language. The volunteer sits in a wheelchair and keeps their eyes closed. Derren asks them to raise their hand when they feel something touching them. Derren touches the doll in different and clearly visible locations including the forehead. The implication is that the volunteer is feeling a touch in the same places. Derren is simply asking the volunteer to raise their hand when they feel a touch. The reality is that there is a gimmick in the wheelchair that is (for example) tapping the spectator on the back whenever Derren taps the doll. We can see that when Derren taps the doll's forehead the spectator apparently feels the same thing, but the use of language ("raise your hand when you feel a touch.... here") means that the volunteer (who has his eyes closed) assumes Derren is touching the doll on the back. The audience believes the volunteer is feeling a touch on the forehead. Since there is no way something could touch the volunteer on the forehead without the audience seeing, we assume there's something weird going on and our attention is drawn away from the wheelchair they forced him to sit in.

When Derren positions the spectator sideways on to the audience and hands him a blackboard and chalk the use of language is again important. Derren explains quite clearly that something will be taking the control of his left arm, "a feeling that is not coming from you". Derren is clear in all his contact with the volunteer in this section using phrases like "did it feel like you were controlling your own arm?" and "you will feel a weight lifting" which shows that there is a gimmick controlling his left arm. We can see the spectator is in a darkened area of the stage and the language used tells the spectator not to be scared and to play along as something moves his arm for him. He writes the simple letters D and S which matches the handkerchief. Whilst it is impossible for me to say with absolute certainty what's going on here, we can be sure that something is taking control of his arm. Maybe again something in the chair is gimmicked – or maybe something as simple as a hidden stagehand dressed in black is moving his arm.

The following routine involves Derren sticking a needle through the skin on the back of the spectator's hand. This routine is not as difficult as it might seem. He starts by asking the volunteer to put his hand on the table with fingers outstretched. By rubbing the back of the doll hand Derren implies that what he's doing is making the volunteer move his fingers back together against his will. Try this yourself; you'll feel that the longer you leave your hand outstretched the more your muscles try to move your fingers back together. It just happens. Don't try the next part at home but trust me when I tell you that if you bunch the skin on the back of your hand and push a needle through there will be no feeling and no blood, again it just happens. But yeah, if you try that at home you're an idiot! Don't do it.

Balloons Finale.

As with previous shows, the finale is a combination of a number of different magical principles combining into one large effect that defies explanation. With the benefit of having taken part in this show live and also watching the TV broadcast we can dissect a number of different processes, distractions and areas where misdirection all play their part. In order to understand what is going on we will need to break the effect down into its component parts, and work backwards from the end. Watching the performance before reading further is important because knowing what happens next will help explain the process. For example, at the end of the show, Derren reveals a huge painted banner revealing spectators chosen numbers. Knowing this is going to appear means the numbers chosen by the spectators need to be forced to match the banner.

Abby, a volunteer celebrating their birthday is brought onto the stage. Many balloons are dropped from the ceiling and blown into the audience. Abby grabs one for herself and all the rest of the balloons are held by audience members. Three of them are randomly picked from the audience by Abby, so we can be confident that all the volunteers are genuinely randomly chosen. However, Derren tells Abby to choose three volunteers with three different colours of balloon. As they come onto the stage, Derren directs them to sit in the three chairs. This is important, because Derren directs the three volunteers to sit specifically where he tells them to. It looks like there are only three colours of balloon, so the specific people don't matter – it's a random choice of volunteers but the balloons will be one of each colour and Derren seats them in the order Blue, Red, Yellow, which is important later on. The balloons contain raffle tickets with random numbers on, but we'll see how every yellow balloon contains the same number as every other yellow balloon, so by restricting the choice of volunteers to one of each balloon colour we'll get the same numbers on stage every night. We're getting ahead of ourselves now because the raffle tickets are not even mentioned at the moment. Also Abby has a free choice of balloon for herself, but we'll see later how this balloon isn't actually used in the show at all, we just remember she has a balloon and our memory plays tricks if we try to work the routine out later. Abby's balloon is a complete red-herring.

Audience members wrote numbers on pieces of paper in the interval, and Derren walks into the centre of the audience and asks the dress circle to throw the papers into a basket. When there are a few numbers in the basket Derren returns to the stage. However Derren is in complete control of this basket all the time it takes to get back to the stage. Similarly to other props used in other shows, this basket can also have a secret compartment which could be switched into place on the way back to the stage. Derren starts off holding a basket full of numbers picked by the audience, but when he gets back to the stage the compartments have been switched and the only slips remaining are the ones Derren always uses, each being the correct number and colour to complete the trick.

Derren then asks Abby to take a paper from the basket and throw it to someone on the front row. Derren makes it clear in the language and presentation that there needs to be space between the volunteers. What he's actually doing is ensuring the numbers land in the correct order. When he sees that the Red paper has been taken from the basket he ensures it is thrown to the left of the stage. What this means is that whatever order she picks the numbers, the result will be in the order Red Yellow Green and Blue. Now we know that Derren placed the tickets in the basket compartment himself we also know that the number formed by these slips is the one he needs for the trick and isn't random at all. It's 1499, which also matches the number of people in the venue. (It's also unlikely that the venue actually does have the exact number of seats Derren refers to, after all who's going to check?)

The three volunteers are now presented with a table containing 36 wooden blocks. These blocks are shown in rows, 1 – 9 in green, red, blue and yellow. Derren is about to give the volunteers a free choice to make a 4 digit number using one block of each colour. Before they do this Derren shows a slide projected onto the back wall which explains the experiment that they are about to recreate. Derren once more explains that there are 1499 audience members (he really wants you to know and remember that number doesn't he?) and then explains the TARG experiment. Conducted on 25th February 1968 with 9027 participants, eagle eyed viewers who've seen the show know that these numbers are going to come into play later – specifically the date (written as 2502), the year (1968) and participants (9027). As with the finale to Enigma, if the viewer knows that these numbers are the key to the whole ending, they can work backwards to puzzle out how the volunteers are going to be forced into choosing the same numbers when they use the wooden blocks.

The wooden blocks are turned face down, and Derren explains that the volunteers will use the blocks to randomly make a four digit number each, hopefully matching the number that is being held by the four spectators sat in the audience. This is a red herring – the numbers they chose will not be matching the audience numbers, but they will form the basis for something much more complicated.

Before the blocks are used, Derren writes on a sheet of card the odds of the numbers matching. He claims the odds are one in 280,063,590,219. Again, these numbers are significant, because if you stack them on top of each other with 219 on top and 280 on the bottom they read like this:

2   1   9

5   9   0

0   6   3

2   8   0

Reading downwards we can see that the first column matches the date on the slide, the second column is the year and the third matches the number of participants taking into account the three volunteers on stage. This again demonstrates that the numbers chosen by volunteers cannot be random because they have to tie in to these numbers on the slide and the card.

The volunteers pick a red block, then yellow, then green and finally blue. The remaining cubes are covered with a black cloth to get them out of view. What's important to realise now is that whilst the three volunteers are making a random four digit number each, none of them know what the number they are making is, until Derren reveals it later. This is extremely important because we can clearly see they really do have a free choice and we've seen that the blocks really do have the 1 – 9 number range in each colour. Our volunteers have made a 4 digit number each, but before these numbers are revealed Derren needs to secretly change them to the numbers he needs – the ones that correspond to the numbers written on the card earlier and also those displayed on the slide behind them.

It's starting to get complicated, isn't it?

I have two explanations for how Derren changes the numbers on the cubes to the numbers he needs. You see, when I saw this show in the live theatre the routine was different to the way it's performed on the TV. The live show I saw was one of the first performances in a long tour and I felt this part of the show was the weakest because what he did looked like a magic conjuring trick. We know the basis of all these routines is magic trickery, but this was the first time I'd seen Derren do something that looked like a traditional magic trick. To me it seemed obvious what was going on, and I suspect that Derren may have felt the same way because later in the tour this section changed to the way it was performed on the TV, and the newer presentation is wonderful – and I'm sorry to say I only have educated guesswork for the broadcast version.

To explain, when I saw the show live the volunteers were asked to choose each cube in the same way you see on the TV broadcast, but instead of merely putting them to the front of the table, Derren gave each volunteer a metal rectangular tube and the volunteers put the cubes in the tube one at a time. The reason this looked like a magic performance is that the cubes and tubes are a magic trick I've seen before many times. Inside the apparently empty tube there is a concealed outer shell that fits closely over the cube that drops in. When Derren reveals the four figure number by lifting off the outer tube what remains on the table is the four cubes chosen by the volunteer, each one with the shell around it. For example, the tube given to the first volunteer contains the shells for 2, 5, 0 and 2. Whichever numbers are selected and placed in the tube can be revealed in a stack 2502. It does not matter which cubes the spectator chooses, they will be revealed to show the numbers Derren wants.

So how is he doing it now? On the TV broadcast there are no tubes! Derren appears to cleanly pick up each cube to reveal the chosen number. We can be sure that he's changing the number from whichever was chosen to the number he needs. Derren picks up each block with a very quick movement and something doesn't look right. We know the blocks have a number printed on one side and the question mark printed on the opposite side. The volunteers put the blocks on the table with the number facing the bottom. He's very fast and very smooth, but something isn't right here – take a close look at the cubes and you can see that he turns the cube to show the number side more times than he needs to. Also most of the moments where he actually lifts the cube involve a cutaway to the crowd. I have no idea exactly how this works, but if you watch the last column of blocks and see how he turns the green block around it looks like he is showing you the same side that had the question mark earlier. All we can be sure of is that these are not fixed solid cubes – perhaps there are hidden flaps or hinges, or a mechanism where a hidden digit is released when needed. We can't be sure exactly what is happening here, but we know that these numbers are not the numbers selected by the volunteers, and of course no-one is questioning this because the volunteers never knew the numbers they chose anyway!

You can see that now these blocks have been stacked up they match the dates and details on the slide, and also on the card that was thrown into the audience earlier.

The three volunteers are then seen to pop their balloons to reveal in order the same numbers they stacked with their blocks. Whilst we know that they were sat in the correct order, I'd assume that each coloured balloon contains the same digits as the other balloons of that colour. By getting one of each colour on stage earlier and forcing them to the correct seats it's easy to make the balloon ticket numbers also match.

Remember the birthday girl? She's still on stage with her balloon. Some theatrics follow where a trick appears to have gone wrong before audience members point out a balloon has got stuck in the staging above the performer's heads. Derren climbs to the top of the stage set and retrieves a balloon caught up there. This isn't an accident of course, it happens every time, but the stuck balloon is passed down to Abby who reads the raffle ticket from inside. It says "Happy Birthday, but we still don't know the secret number". The four audience members shout out their numbers to reveal 1499, which matches the number on the raffle ticket, and the banner revealed that Derren climbs down on. We know from the earlier description how this number was forced, but it is interesting to note that in this presentation Abby's balloon was merely a distraction and isn't actually needed in the trick at all! The matching number was inside the other balloon so there was no random chance – the numbers matched all along.

Infamous.

The Show.

Infamous changed the format of the shows again, moving away from traditional magic even further, with a second half of the show devoted to hypnosis and a spectacular demonstration of Psychic Surgery. The show had the feel of previous live performances but ramped up the standard of presentation to further drive the illusion that the performer is a genuine miracle worker rather than a mere magician. This continues into the next live show, Miracle, and there are many similarities between the two. There is a huge amount of top quality material in this show, so let's dive right in.

Opening.

An example of some of the techniques used by mediums and cold readers begins, with Derren using general information about the demographic of his audience to select a volunteer from the crowd. He asks for every lady in the audience to stand, then whittles the group down by specifying an age, and the first initial. A lady named Fay is chosen. Derren asks questions, eventually asking the volunteer to tell him the name of one of her dogs, and Derren will read her mind and find out the name of the other. This has to be pre-show work as there's no way he can deduce the information from the questions asked. Whether the pre-show work is done in advance by researching booking names or address details of ticket sales, or is as simple as asking an audience member for the information in the foyer – it looks like a miracle to the audience, but Derren simply knew the information and used questioning to eliminate the rest of the audience and leave only the spectator he wanted.

A man called Nick thinks of an English word. This will be a completely random choice as Nick is allowed to change his mind as many times as he likes. Nick has to write the word on a piece of paper and an usher will provide a clipboard with a piece of paper on. This could be done with something as simple as a piece of carbon paper, so the crew member can look at the clipboard off-stage and see what the word was. There are also very expensive clipboards available from magic dealers which transmit a copy of what has been written or drawn to a tablet computer hidden in the wings. Anyone who writes a word on one of these clipboards can have their word (or drawing) guessed by a mind reader who can simply look at the hidden screen and read the word.

Another volunteer writes their mobile phone number on a piece of paper, this is folded up and put in her pocket. It would only require a simple piece of carbon paper, or the aforementioned clipboard to ensure that the crew member who is holding the clipboard would now have a copy of the phone number to use later in the show. Of course, by the time we get to that point the audience will have forgotten that the volunteer wrote the number on a piece of paper.

Derren is at pains to ensure that the volunteer does not react when Derren states the word is 'Film". This is because the audience volunteer has not thought of this word and the trick appears to be going wrong. The volunteer is brought onto the stage and Derren even comments that the expression on his face makes him believe the trick has gone wrong. The volunteer isn't allowed to react at all to the reveal of the word, he simply opens the envelope and it's at this point that a spot of dual reality comes into play. The volunteer is wondering how the word he wrote on the piece of paper has changed into the word 'Film'. This is achieved by a simple envelope switch, or maybe a gimmicked envelope. But whilst the volunteer looks impressed by the switch, the audience react to the much bigger trick – because they think the audience member wrote 'Film' on the piece of paper at the start of the trick. He didn't, but the reveal makes everyone think he did, and the trick appears to be a success.

Trance State.

The next section of the show involves a similar demonstration of hypnosis to that seen in the Somnambulism section of the Enigma show. There's not a great deal I can add to that original explanation, it's a wonderful way to choose a volunteer!

The Box and drawing prediction.

The volunteer on the stage places his hand through a hole in the top of a box and is asked to describe the object he can feel inside the box. This is a neat effect in itself, but it's set up at this point to introduce something even more impressive later on. The box is a special gimmicked box that allows the performer to switch the item in the box before it is revealed. In this show, the volunteer is given a teaspoon to feel, and he describes this. When the front of the box is removed the teaspoon has been replaced with a ladle and the similarity of the items makes the audience believe that Adam was feeling the ladle all along. The end of this routine involves a fur glove being switched for a Tarantula spider! Before the interval, The Adam's mum (Christine) was invited onto the stage and asked to draw a picture secretly which is sealed into an envelope. Christine draws a picture, and this will be revealed later. It's very telling that Christine is specifically told not to tell anyone what she drew. "Don't even tell your daughter!"

Derren commands. There's a reason for this, and we'll come to that later.

Psychic Surgery.

We've all seen magicians making playing cards appear as if from nowhere. They show their hands empty, then reach out and pull playing cards out of thin air. We all had a granddad that made coins appear from behind our ears when we were kids. So making a bloody piece of meat appear from the hands isn't that much of a different trick. Psychic Surgery, as Derren points out after this trick, is merely a conjuring trick. My suggestion is that the blood soaked meaty pieces and blood capsules are concealed in Derren's gloves, the white coat or around the frame of the table. The effect of plunging fingers through the skin is simply achieved by miming the act and bending the knuckles at the same time as plunging the hand towards the skin, and opening the hand again when pulling back out. There are entire books written on the subject of Psychic Surgery and this disturbing effect has been presented as real by scam artists in the past.

The Box – part 2.

The Aeroplane in the box is a stunning combination of showmanship, misdirection and outright deception. We can see that a selection of audience members has been brought up onto the stage. It's really important to understand the process with which the group was brought onto the stage. Derren explains that if anyone in the crowd is considering visiting a psychic medium in the near future, he will invite them onto the stage to join the second half of the show. They will be given a unique view of the events of the show. In explaining this, the crowd become Derren's accomplices. It's extremely clever how this part of the show is pitched, because the crowd on stage are primed to expect to see things they would not normally see. The theatre audience see the crowd on stage as validation that the routines can be seen from all angles without giving the game away. This is very significant in the Aeroplane trick because I believe that the audience on stage can see everything that's going on. The hypnotised volunteer is brought around from his hypnotic trance and attention is drawn back to the box frame that was used earlier in the show.

Derren makes very clever use of language and performance in this section. The frame of the box is a trick device and there is a hidden aeroplane that is obscured from our view by Adam's hand. Derren's words (*"You will feel something moving from your mind down towards your fingers"*) tell Adam what he should expect to feel. Adam feels the aeroplane in the box. Audience members behind can see what's going on, but they expect to see this and they are enjoying being in on the secret. Derren asks Adam what he can feel, and steers him by giving him clues. Derren still seems surprised when Adam says he can feel an Aeroplane, and asks more questions to seal the illusion that Derren has no idea what the object will be. Of course Derren knows all along what it is. The object moves back into the hidden place in the frame before Adam removes his hand. Derren then takes the envelope that Christine sealed earlier and opens it up. This reveals the picture that she drew earlier. Except – that's not the picture she drew. I believe this envelope has been gimmicked to open in two ways. Derren unseals the envelope before handing it to Adam, and this means that a pre-drawn picture of an aeroplane is revealed instead of the image Christine drew. So that's two thousand audience members believing that Christine predicted the image correctly, and only Christine herself knowing that the image wasn't the one she drew. At this point, Christine is in the audience, she's not able to blurt anything out! The trick is over, and we quickly move on to the next part.

Oracle Act Revisited.

Derren performs an act of mediumship on the audience members on the stage. For a full explanation of this routine, please read the explanation of the Oracle Act from Evening of Wonders. We can see that the audience members were given cards to fill out with their names, and these are visible on stage in a glass bowl to the left of the stage. I'd wager that these cards also have space to write more details than just the spectator's name, and it is this information that is revealed by Derren. This is presented more from the point of view of a performance of mediumship, but the idea is much the same as the Oracle Act we saw earlier.

Finale.

Derren explains that two years ago he started working on a spectacular feat of memory. He's apparently learned the Complete Works of Shakespeare and also learned a number of books worth of bus timetables. The remaining volunteers gather around a table where each audience member has a dice and a bowl. Two Rubik's Cubes are handed out into the audience. An audience member is asked to write down a ten digit number. (Phew – that's a lot of stuff going on at once!).

The volunteers are asked to pick up the dice from the bowls. They do not roll them until around thirty seconds later, when Derren is ready to write the numbers on the board. I believe these dice are loaded with a magnet and the table itself is magnetised. The magnet in the table is remote controlled, allowing the dice to be rolled multiple times with random results, but once the table is switched on the dice will always land in the correct way. The result looks random, but the number is the same every night. This means that Derren doesn't need to memorise every single bus timetable, he only needs to learn bus route 463. The presentation here is awesome, because Derren explains the memory technique he uses to memorise the bus routes. This method is explained in his book, Trick of the Mind. But whilst he explains this technique (and even gets one of the bus stops slightly wrong for effect), it's fun to know that he's not actually needing to use the technique he's telling us about – he only needed to learn the one route, and he can use any memory technique he likes when it's only one route.

The Complete Works of Shakespeare is used in a very convincing way. Derren uses the number that was generated to tell us the contents of page 264. Of course, we now know that Derren will only need to memorise the contents of that one page because the number generated wasn't random. But how does he then go on to ask the volunteer to name any page number? That has to be random, so how can he do it? This is a very clever version of a trick known as a Book Test. These (expensive) books look like ordinary books, but the words on the pages are gimmicked to allow the performer to perform the effect. One famous example is a novel that upon casual inspection reads like a regular story. However, if you sit down and read the book from cover to cover, you start to notice that the story makes very little sense. It has no actual plot or characters to speak of. The entire story is written using only 26 significant words, with short words to pad out the list into real sentences. If I asked you to choose a good, interesting word from the sentence "The man went to the photocopier and looked at the small indentations on the page", then you will surely choose photocopier or indentations. And all 26 words used in the book start with a different letter of the alphabet, so the magician can tell you what word you are thinking of by simply asking you what the first letter is. The Complete Works of Shakespeare has a number of gimmicks in the writing, but one of these allows the performer to know the first and last words of the page by only knowing the page number. This is a completely unnecessary extra bit for the routine as the first page number was forced so the magician could have used any book. By using the trick book as well it adds another convincer for anyone who thinks the number on the blackboard was forced. If Derren merely had remembered the contents of just one page of the book, how could he possibly have known the random page suggested by the volunteer? Well, now you know.

And what about the grains of rice from the bowl? Derren has the correct number of rice grains concealed upon his person. I suggest that he takes the rice into his right hand as he turns his back on the audience. The talcum powder is a distraction as he goes into the audience. They can see no rice is hidden in the bottle of talc. But when he turns to go back on the stage, he can secrete the rice in his right hand, then pretend to remove it from the bowl later.

As for the amazing finale moment, how did Derren make two apparently random numbers add up to match the volunteer's phone number? We know that Derren's crew already know the phone number because the audience member wrote it down at the beginning of the show. Was there carbon paper on the clipboard, or was it a trick clipboard that transmitted the image to an offstage screen? Whichever method he uses, the only variable is the man in the audience who wrote down a 10 digit number. Derren's crew know that the number on the blackboard will be 46326422. They need to subtract this from the phone number obtained earlier, and write this on a card. We can only assume that the person in the audience who reads out the ten digit number was not the one who chose the number and the cards were switched. Or perhaps, when Derren explained that he would be asked to write down a ten digit number, the stagehand with the pen and paper dictated the number to him. No-one said that the man would have a free choice of ten digit number. We just assumed that. So the pre-planned number on the blackboard is added to the forced number from the audience member and it adds up to the telephone number we knew from the beginning of the show. Easy? No, this is world class performance.

And the Rubik's Cubes? Derren's cube is a cube that has been solved, then has a small, pre-learned series of twists to make it look completely messed up. When the audience volunteer hands the cube back to Derren he slips a shell over the cube. The shell is painted to match the pattern on Derren's cube.

Miracle.

The Show.

Over the course of 2015, Derren and his team presented his most audacious show to date. Miracle was a celebration of the work Derren has performed in previous live shows, with similar methods and routines in the first half. Leading up to the finale, the bulk of the show focussed on an expose of faith healing, which was appeared to be misunderstood by many after the television broadcast of this live show. In debunking faith healing Derren showed that anyone could achieve the illusion of being a faith healer and the power of positive thinking can overcome the feeling of sickness, albeit for a short time. Following the broadcast, Derren trended on Twitter, with many commentators missing the point entirely, believing that Derren Brown was actually trying to show that he did have healing powers, and others who had attended the live shows commenting that they still felt cured. Faith healing is nonsense, and in the live show, Derren demonstrated this, doing it so well that it would be easy to believe that Derren does have a psychic gift. The TV broadcast concentrated on the psychic healing in the second half of the show, and it seemed to me that a great deal more of the magical content was cut out of the broadcast. In fact, my favourite part of the show (a more traditional magic effect) was cut out entirely, but I'm going to list that part of the routine anyway because it was awesome. By removing a large proportion of the magic for the TV broadcast and focussing on the psychic healing, I think the overall spirit of debunking psychics is lost in the TV version and I suspect the heavily edited content of the TV broadcast contributed to the feeling that Derren was demonstrating his powers, rather than debunking the scam.

The Inflatable Balloon Prediction.

The Miracle TV broadcast begins with Derren handing out two pieces of paper to people in the audience. A Balloon is thrown into the audience and the random audience member who catches it chooses a character, in this case, Mickey Mouse. The audience members with the pieces of paper are asked to do the same thing. This starts off three games of consequences being played at the same time, one by the people holding the inflatable ball being passed around the audience, and two being played by the audience members with the pens and paper. In the TV broadcast the routine ends with a game of consequences written on flip chart paper on stage:

Mickey Mouse, holding a pencil sharpener, sitting on a dog bed saying "G'day campers!"

Derren has presented this as a mind control experiment, and we are meant to believe that the audience members are not given a free choice, but are somehow being controlled to say the words he wants them to say. The climax to this routine is that the balloon will be popped and the chosen words revealed to have been inside the balloon all along. Derren does everything he can to persuade the audience members that he is putting the word into their heads. Psychologically, this means that Derren already knows the words and will know instantly when a volunteer doesn't say the word he expects. This is used to great effect as he mutters "never mind" when the volunteer says Dog Bed, a lovely little convincer which will sell the illusion of mind control a little later when he is revealed to have predicted this one incorrectly. (When Derren reveals that there is a prediction inside the balloon, and he will indeed have written Sun Bed instead of Dog Bed.)

The other two consequences lists are passed from the audience members to the volunteer who takes them onto the stage whilst still holding the inflatable.   When I saw this live, an usher took the inflatable from the audience member in order to help her get out of her seat. I expect that the usher was writing the "predictions" on a piece of paper during the previous presentation and slides the paper inside the balloon as he took it from the audience member. Also, the two consequences games that are played by the other audience members would need to be switched, either at this point, or by Derren himself as they are handled on stage for the first time. It's important to understand that it makes no difference what the audience members wrote because by the time we get to see, both papers have been switched. The game of consequences we will see is not one that was written by either of the two groups in the audience, but by having two pieces of paper in play, each group will assume that the other group's page is the one being used.

The two audience consequences games are handed to Derren, and he takes one of them, unfolds it and checks that all the information they will need has been written correctly. On checking the first piece of paper, Derren sees that everything is OK and the second piece is put into his pocket and forgotten about. Again, this sells the idea to everyone who contributed to the two consequences games that what they wrote is on the paper in Derren's pocket. In fact, the piece of paper still in play contains the specific words Derren and his team need for the finale, and no-one in the audience contributed to this.

The "audience" contribution is read out – "Private Court Blender" is the headline, followed by the story that reads "Camilla Parker-Bowles holding a small dog sits on a cucumber and says "You've grown since I last saw you!".

As Derren writes out the contents of the paper onto a flipchart, this forms a prediction that will be used at the end of the show, and is not going to be referred to in the next part of the current routine. It's important to remember that in the real live show this reveal will be a full two and a half hours from now and the audience will have forgotten the specifics of where these words came from. The audience believes these words were randomly picked by audience members, and the actual audience members that wrote the words are assuming that *their* words are in Derren's pocket and the paper by the other volunteers is in use.

The volunteer is prompted to pop the balloon to reveal that there is another piece of paper inside, and this contains the prediction that Derren made earlier. In order to convince the audience that this is no mere trick, Derren is not entirely correct in his prediction, revealing that he predicted Mickey Mouse holding a pencil sharpener, sitting on a sun bed, saying "G'day campers!". We can assume that the usher inserted the "prediction" into the balloon after the audience had made their random guesses but before it was brought on stage, and deliberately having one wrong (but close) answer is a brilliant little piece of subtlety. If the prediction inside the balloon had matched exactly with the audience suggestions, this may lead people to believe that he must have got the prediction in the balloon after the audience had made their guesses, which we now know is exactly what we think happened! By getting one of the guesses wrong, but still being very close (Dog Bed became Sun Bed) we are left with the feeling that this was not a mere magic trick, but was really an attempt at mind control. How did Derren make the audience members say what he wanted them to say, when they all gave apparently free choices? The answer is they were free choices, and whatever they said is what is inserted into the balloon after they were chosen.

Eating a Light Bulb.

In the TV broadcast, a huge chunk of great content was skipped at this point (see the chocolate game later in this book), and we rejoin the show with a new volunteer, Sarah, sitting at a dinner table. Derren asks the volunteer to remove the light bulb from a lamp, wrap it in a napkin, smash it with a hammer, and open the napkin to show the shards of the broken glass. Derren emphasises that the glass is real, solid, sharp, and dangerous. Derren slowly and carefully has a piece of the glass put onto his tongue and he describes how it feel s to have the glass in his mouth, referring to sharp sections of the glass cutting into the soft palate of the mouth. However he goes on to eat the glass, much to the shock and disgust of the audience. Again, we see another great example of the power of presentation over content, as Derren discusses the danger, the potential lawsuits, and the importance of following instructions to the letter as the volunteer is instructed how to eat the glass shards of the light bulb. We hear the crunch of the glass as Sarah takes a bite. Derren instructs Sarah to chew pieces of apple at the same time as she eats the glass, and advises that she will feel a sandy mulch as the apple surrounds the glass. Again, this is all an extraordinary exercise in presentation and performance.

We have to assume that a national touring theatrical performance, using audience participation would be simply unable to perform a routine like this if there was any danger involved. Also, the TV broadcast states not to try this at home, but the performance implies that if followed to the letter, you would be able to safely eat the glass just as Sarah did. Let's look at this situation rationally. You cannot safely eat glass. Even if you could use apple to mask sharp edges, you would have no control of the glass as it travels through the throat and into the stomach. It would be a much more sensible approach for the performer to use light bulbs made of sugar-glass, which can be made specifically for the performance, or purchased from magic dealers!

Grabbing a coin from a volunteer's hand.

There's not a great deal we can say about this section. Everything you see is exactly as it happens. Indeed, you can watch this a couple of times from the TV broadcast, and see where Derren looks, points, and how he uses his body language and speech to fool the volunteer into allowing Derren to grab the coins. The first five coin grabs are exactly as you see on TV and you can perform this routine on friends and family by practicing doing what Derren does. On the sixth attempt, the coin is placed into the volunteers hand but this is not the coin that the spectator thinks it is. As all focus is on Derren's attempts to steal the coin, a commemorative silver coin has been placed in the spectators hand instead of the real coin used earlier. Derren has the 50p coin palmed in his hand and as he comes in to steal the coin from the spectator we believe that he has been so quick that he managed to steal the 50p from the spectator and replace it with the commemorative coin. In reality, the coin was already in the spectator's hand and the 50p was already in Derren's hand before he went in for the steal.

The Nail Stab Trick.

A few years ago, the Nail Stab was a hugely popular trick among magicians, until stories started to be told of magicians that had incurred serious injury from performing it wrong. There are multiple variations on this trick, but all involve a choice where the magician slams their palm quickly onto a paper cup, paper bag or similar object that may contain a large, very sharp spike. Tension rises as one by one, the choices are eliminated, and the magician ends up with only two choices on the table. After they slam their hand down for the last time, they reveal the last choice remaining did indeed have the dangerous spike concealed within. And this is a trick that can, and does go wrong.

As the volunteer carelessly knocks one of the nail bags' from the table, Derren picks it up and remarks that the volunteer is clumsy. We know that in a Derren Brown show, nothing can be left to chance and nothing can be allowed to happen that could prevent the routine working. I saw the show twice to be sure that the "clumsy cow" (as she will be referred to later) knocks the bag onto the floor every time. In fact, on close inspection we can see on the TV broadcast that the bag mysteriously falls on its own... as if by magic. The volunteer thinks she knocked over the bag but it wasn't her fault.

As I mentioned earlier, The Nail Stab trick is notorious among magicians. The simple method requires concentration and under the theatre lights it can be easy to misremember the method. Derren's genius in presentation is to show clips of the trick being done wrongly and the injury and chaos that ensue. There are many examples of the Nail Stab being performed badly on YouTube, and the trick was heavily featured in an E4 documentary, "When Magic Tricks Go Wrong". One example had a magician holding the spectators hand and slamming it down on the nail and this resulted in a serious injury for the innocent volunteer.

There are multiple methods for this routine, and a variety of presentations. The first of these that I actively tried involved five circular wooden bases, one of which had the sharp spike hammered through. Polystyrene cups were placed over each of the bases, resulting in 5 identical looking constructs. When the magician knows where to look, they can identify that a simple indentation in the base allows the cups to stand inside the ridge and one of the indentations is thicker than the rest. The magician can identify this one and of course, the different base shape is the one that houses the spike. I believe that this mindset, the understanding that the magician knows "it's that one, it's that one", combined with the pressure of performance can lead the magician to slam their hand down onto the spike in error. Psychologically the brain is telling them which base is the important one, and this leads the magician to focus their mindset there. In the heat of the moment, it's not surprising that some magicians have lost focus, gone with that feeling and slammed down on the spike.

It's an incredibly powerful effect and one that I wouldn't dare perform myself, especially when bringing a spectator's hand into the effect! I wouldn't want to be involved in that lawsuit. It's no surprise that after a while, new versions of this effect were devised by magicians that allow for the same presentation without the danger. The genius in Derren's presentation is in showing the audience the examples of where the original versions of the Nail Trick caused injury, then performing a more modern, safer version. As with the light bulb eating earlier, I doubt any touring theatre production would be able to get the insurance to perform the dangerous version of this trick with a real volunteer.

In the version Derren performs each paper bag contains a wooden base and a nail, but the nail lays flat. Derren shows one of the bags and in the process of reaching inside, the nail is stood upright into the base and removed and shown to the audience. The nail is replaced into the bag and when obscured from view the nail is removed from the wood and laid flat. This makes the trick completely safe, and at the end of the performance, the remaining bag is opened, the magician reaches in, slides the nail into an upright position and removes it from the bag. As there was a base and nail in each bag, it doesn't matter which bags the volunteer chose, and the chances are that this nail is not the same nail, or bag that was shown at the beginning of the trick. Remember that during this routine, although the volunteer mixed the bags up, Derren chose the order when he smashed his hands down onto them. This is important because after the commercial break, Derren makes a point of explaining that the volunteer chose to put the nail in bag number three. In reality Derren can make the nail appear in any bag, and Derren slams down his hands on the other bags in every performance, leaving the bag in the third position. When he talks about the significance of the third position after the commercial break, he is simply adding further misdirection by telling the audience it was the volunteer who chose that position.

Faith Healing.

Derren performed (and explained) faith healing in the TV Special, Miracles for Sale. There have been entire books written just on this subject. Around the world, faith healing has been used as a legitimate medical tool for many years, which can be devastating to those who believe in it. Along with psychics, mediums and the like, Derren debunks faith healing in such a clear and obvious way that it's difficult to see why so many people around the world believe in it. Faith healing is a complex magical performance, involving traditional methods of making things appear and disappear but presented in a medical, not magical environment.

Through the power of suggestion, cheesy music and bright (and extremely hot) lights, Derren invites the audience to join in, using positive phrases, "this is your one chance and you will be very pleased that you did", and a number of audience members make their way to the stage steps. Derren explains that he does not believe in any of what he's doing but he invites the audience members onto the stage one at a time. Derren uses a combination of hypnosis, cold reading and mentalism effects to perform similar miracles to those of the faith healers. Many people come to the stage steps but only six make it to the stage. He explains in the finale of the show how the positivity, bright lights and a belief that there really is a healing sweeping across the room, the symptoms can simply go away. This seems to be a genuine explanation (and if you've read his brilliant book, Happy, you'll know that there is so much power in belief, positive thinking and attitude) that those pains and symptoms can often just go away.

That's not to say that every effect in this section of the show is achieved this way. When I saw this performed live, there were a huge number of people heading for the stage, but only six appeared in the performance. I was aware that the ushers were standing at the front of the stage and were speaking to the volunteers. There are many ways that the ushers could collate information and pass it to the performer un-noticed. We have already discussed the use of technology where Bluetooth is used to transmit writing from a clipboard to a tablet device, for example.

The first volunteer, Gertie, is asked to reveal the information about herself, which gives a window of time for the research to be done on the other volunteers. While Gertie is on stage, no information is proactively revealed by Derren.

I was recently made aware of a speaker system that fires the sound into a specific spot which could be used for this routine. When the performer stands on the mark on stage they can hear the sound of the speaker, yet the person next to them would not be able to hear it. This can be used to provide information to the performer that would traditionally been done with an earpiece.

The second volunteer is on stage for some time and it appears that Derren reveals a lot of information, but the only thing that differs between the two volunteers is that Derren tells Shannon that she has a knee injury. The rest of this volunteer's experience is showmanship. We cannot tell if the information about the knee was fed to Derren in advance, but this is one method, another being what is known as cold-reading. The other volunteers reveal the information about themselves, with Derren merely asking the questions. The only remaining volunteer on stage to have a more specific reading is Sam, which again could be fed to the performer from the usher, or an example of cold reading.

Cold Reading.

The best book to learn about cold reading is by Ian Rowland, and can be bought from his website. The Full Facts Book of Cold Reading covers a multitude of ways that psychics, mediums and fortune tellers convince us that they have knowledge of our lives, our loved ones and our futures. If you visit a medium in pursuit of contacting a loved one, you will often hear statements that sound specific to your situation but on reflection the words could apply to anyone. If a medium was to remind you of the pet that sleeps in the hallway, the elderly man in uniform, or the box of very old photographs, these would all sound like they knew something about you personally, but most people have a box of old photographs, a grandparent in the war or a family pet. There are many great examples that cold readers use, but many of these involve the knee (a very common complaint, especially when talking to an audience member who walks with a slight limp), the chest and heart, the shoulders and head. Suggesting to a larger, overweight person that they may have experienced chest or heart problems will usually get a positive response. Notice how the use of language remains vague – to say "heart problems" is far less specific than, say, "heart-attack". Also, the performer does not necessarily end their sentence unless it gains a reaction, and adapts what they say to the response of the volunteer. Notice that when Derren says that Sam has a pain in his chest, Sam reacts and Derren does not continue to talk about other parts of the body. Derren may have been about to say "the chest, and shoulders" but stops as Sam reacts. Sam also says his chest is filled with butterflies, and may be describing the feeling of being on stage in front of so many people, but Derren says, "That's what I was talking about there" and makes these nerves appear to be another example of the healing powers.

Cold reading is a fascinating subject, and I recommend reading further.

Give me Strength.

More traditional magical performance is combined with the healing performance for added effect. Sam is invited to lift a very heavy suitcase. It appears to be just an ordinary suitcase, but it is a heavily gimmicked magical prop. The suitcase appears to be full of bricks, and Sam cannot lift it off the ground even an inch. One of the bricks is removed from the case in order to demonstrate that these are in fact, real bricks. In fact, the suitcase is impossible to lift until the performer allows it. This could be achieved through use of strong magnets. Whatever the method, the volunteer's strength has not been affected – no-one could have lifted the suitcase until the magnet is deactivated, or whatever trickery is employed.

When Derren address the audience by telling them that someone has tinnitus that has just gone, this causes the audience to address what he is saying. Could he be referring to me? Tinnitus is an awful condition that leaves a sound in the ears. For many this comes and goes. Sufferers tend to tune out the sound as it is something they have to live with. In an audience so large, there is bound to be someone in the audience that has tinnitus and the simple mention of it causes any sufferers to suddenly think about it. This is enough for someone to believe, if only for a few minutes that they have been cured.

When Derren approaches Kim from the audience, he picks her specifically, and describes her neck complaint, and asks how long she has experienced the pain. This lady appears randomly chosen, but she would have been up at the front of the stage earlier, and have spoken to the ushers. Therefore this encounter is done in the same way as Shannon's on-stage, but is presented in a different way as it is conducted in the audience.

A spectator is asked to scribble on a piece of paper. The spectator is blindfolded, so when they look at the paper afterwards they have no way of knowing whether the scribbles they can see are actually drawn by them. What if the paper already had scribbles on, and the pen was empty? Heat sensitive ink or paper can be used which disappears when heated by the candle. By writing the message in regular ink, then scribbling over it in heat sensitive ink the effect can be achieved. Again, if this audience member spoke to an usher earlier, the team would know about Chris' hernia, and could write that on the paper in advance.

When the performer reveals that God is healing someone's eyesight, Derren would need to locate anyone in the audience with glasses to achieve this effect. Derren appears to take a brochure from someone in the crowd, but by showing a gimmicked brochure with deliberately unclear writing on one page and large clear print on another, this effect can be achieved. Derren shows one volunteer page four of the programme and she cannot read it without her glasses. The programme is closed, and reopened after the faith healing has taken place. Perhaps the brochure has been printed with the words "fuck me sideways" in large clear letters. This would explain why when Derren says "Can you read this, here?" and points to the page, the audience volunteer gets such a great audience reaction. The audience thinks she is amazed that her eyesight has been restored, but she could be simply reading the bad language. If you listen to the way she speaks, you can hear that she is not giving a genuine shocked reaction by her tone of voice. This suggests that the programme was reopened at a different page with different words and larger print. The same method could also be used to remove the other volunteer's eyesight on stage, as the brochure is reopened at a doctored page of gibberish.

Finale.

After warning the many spectators that came onto the stage not to throw away pills (because after all, Derren is showing us how faith healing is a sham), we move into the finale section of the show, and this is the point, as with previous shows, where smaller, forgotten details from earlier in the show come back into play. The live audience at this stage has forgotten that there were two games of consequences played at the beginning of the show. We never did see a reason for the Camilla Parker-Bowles story did we?

As with previous shows, the ending we see is superseded by something much bigger. Derren apparently makes a watch stop with the power of his mind, although I suspect this is a gimmicked watch, available from magic dealers which can be stopped at will, either by remote control or by a mechanism squeezed by the magician as he holds it by the buckle.

Also the TV edit butchers the content of this show so much that we never saw the audience member being handed an envelope at the beginning of the show, but now Derren takes that back at this stage and takes a copy of the Daily Mail from within. He shows us that the first page of the newspaper contains the words "Private Court Blender". We covered earlier that this piece of paper was apparently written randomly by audience members but was switched with one written by Derren's team. All they needed to do was to buy the newspaper, and choose the page with the most interesting details. We also know that during the Nail Stab trick the bag is always knocked off the table by a "clumsy cow", and as nothing in the show is left to chance, it is easy for the team to place an advert in the personal ad section of the newspaper stating as such! In the theatrical performances I saw they used local newspapers (Manchester Evening News and Liverpool Echo). Once all the theatre dates and venues were confirmed, it must have been someone's job to book the adverts with each paper on the appropriate dates.

Chocolate game: (not featured in TV broadcast).

I wanted to include the chocolate game from Miracle as a great example of magical thinking. Sadly, this was not featured in the TV broadcast but I hope this may appear as a DVD extra. The presentation was wonderful with the entire back of the stage displayed as a projection of a contents card from the inside of a box of Quality Street chocolates. The audience can clearly see the whole range of chocolates in a Quality Street box, with the names, colours and appearance of each one. The routine involved

Derren explaining that he can tell the choice of a chocolate from the box by concentrating on the sound of the chocolate being unwrapped and chewed. Audience members were allowed to choose a chocolate from the box, then a microphone was held to their mouths as they unwrapped and chewed them. Derren got every guess correctly.

The reason that this is a great example of magical thinking is because the theory of what you are seeing is actually based on a card trick, known as the Tossed Out Deck. In that trick a pack of cards is wrapped in elastic bands and thrown to an audience volunteer. They peel the pack apart and look at one card within the pack. The pack remains in the elastic bands so it can be thrown to another audience member who does the same, then a third audience member has the pack thrown to them and a final card is chosen. Three people in different parts of the audience now have a chosen card and the pack is thrown back to the performer on stage. The performer then uses mentalism magic to read the minds of the three volunteers and tells them what cards were chosen.

So how does this magic card trick compare with the chocolates trick? The answer relies in a beautiful piece of subtlety in the language used when the cards are named by the performer. At the end of the card trick, the magician tells the three volunteers which cards they chose. If you saw this trick live and were asked to describe what you saw to a friend, you may well misremember what was said, and describe the magician telling the three volunteers which three cards they chose. This is a great example of how the brain fills in the gaps in the routine. The magician actually makes his announcement in a vague sentence that sounds like it contains more specific information than it does. The wording is along these lines.

"Ok, I think I have something, so I would like our three standing volunteers to concentrate on the cards they chose. Yes – it's clear, I have it. Seven of Clubs, Three of Diamonds, and Jack of Spades. If I have named the card you chose, please would you sit down."

All three volunteers sit down and a wonderful piece of dual-reality has just occurred. The audience think that three volunteers picked three cards and the magician named all three correctly. The volunteers believe their mind was read and that the other two cards named must therefore be the cards chosen by the other two volunteers. In fact, the pack only contained those three cards, repeated many times. The elastic band prevented the volunteers looking thought the pack. They opened the deck, looked at one card only. If they did happen to flick to the next card they would see a different card, confirming the belief that this is a regular deck. The important point is the audience remembers that three volunteers were chosen and three cards were named. The magician never specified which card was chosen by which volunteer and the audience's brain fills in the gaps.

This card trick, combined with a little magical thinking works in the same way if you substitute the cards with chocolates, the deck box with a chocolate box and a theatre usher instead of throwing. Instead of identifying the card through mind reading, we identify the chocolate by the sound of the chewing. For a tour of this size, all you need to do is buy many boxes of chocolates, sort them out so that each box only contains three varieties of chocolate, then perform the same routine with three audience volunteers. At the end, the magician says, *"Toffee Penny, Hazelnut Crunch and Coconut Crème. If I have guessed your chocolate correctly, please sit down"*. As the box only contained these three chocolates, each volunteer assumes that their chocolate was guessed correctly, the other two must relate to the other two volunteers, and the audience believes that Derren really can tell a chocolate just by the sound of it being chewed. Magicians however, see something even bigger – a perfect example of how a card trick can be turned into something so much more interesting and impressive though ingenuity and magical thinking.

Underground and Secret

Derren and his team travelled to America and performed his first run of theatre shows outside of the UK. In preparation for this, Derren staged a short run of shows in London, called Derren Brown: Underground. This was tweaked and changed multiple times to create a "best of" show that would be taken to America. Once completed, it was renamed Derren Brown: Secret, and served to establish Derren's talent with a new overseas audience, and received many rave reviews.

Upon his return to the UK, the name was changed back to Underground and it toured across the UK. I was extremely impressed by this performance, having watched Derren grow as an artist over so many years and it was obvious that we were watching the man I consider to be the best performer in this field at the absolute top of his game. Whilst the show contained little new material (all the main events are already covered in this book), every effect was performed with extra polish and showmanship and Derren made the magic seem effortless. Again I listened to the conversations in the bar during the interval and after the show, and the audience was mystified. Many of the crowd were seeing the effects for the first time and were simply blown away. The long standing fans loved seeing the routines again and I'm sure there were some of the die-hard fans appreciating the extra polish and tweaks that had gone into these routines over the years of performance.

Describing the show as a "best of" suggests that the audience is seeing the same routines, but these little changes and small details meant there was even less margin for error as the language used on stage controlled the audience volunteers precisely. Clues that had helped me come up with my theories in the past were often absent. It was a great demonstration of how the magic evolves over so many performances and this is a real lesson for any magician to learn.

All the best artists, whether magicians or otherwise, work hard to create a perfect show that they are proud of. One performer I spoke to gave this a name – he called it, "The Perfect Five Minutes".   His theory was that in creative fields, less is definitely more. We love our favourite music CD that contains 10 great songs far more than the one that has 10 great songs and another 10 lousy ones. We adore the live stage vocalist who hits the notes with absolute perfection much more than the singer that does an adequate job of singing the hundreds of songs they have learned.   Self-editing allows a performer to create their five minute masterpiece (or their ten minute masterpiece, one hour masterpiece and so on), knowing that their work is the best it can be.

I've referred to the kind of magician that practices all their card tricks over and over in the bedroom and forgets to work on their charisma or their persona. In magic, the "Perfect Five Minutes" could be the three tricks that always go down well with the audience, honed to absolute perfection, performed in the best way you know how, getting better with every performance. You show your perfect routine to every crowd in your area. Once you've nailed this, take the performance on tour, travel to every area in your country. When there's nowhere left, jump on a plane and start your world tour. Finally, when your show has been seen by everyone, squander it completely by doing it on television – then come home and start working on your next "Perfect Five Minutes".

Of course, the above applies whether you work a five minute routine or a two hour show. I know magicians who *could* perform a different hour of magic at every wedding they work at but none of them do this. They self-edit, they cut routines down, and create their one perfect hour that makes every wedding day special. They have great routines that they love, yet cast them aside because their experience says that wedding audiences might not like them. Their bulletproof hour of magic gets a fantastic response and they do this over and over again.

In the case of Derren Brown: Underground, we learn an extra valuable piece of information. Even when you have created your perfect routine, there is still room for improvement. Whilst each of the effects has been seen before in previous shows, they have been tweaked, refined and improved over years of live stage performance. No extra tricks were added, routines were not more complicated to the audience, and the proven formula was not spoiled, but the presentation was smoother, audience control was improved, effects were cleaner and no, I still didn't spot the Gorilla.

The routines featured all have their origins in the previous shows and appeared to use the same methods as discussed earlier in the book. Changes were made to create continuity throughout the show, and some of the more traditional magic effects were disguised even more beautifully than before, making the show less of a traditional "magic" performance than ever. For example, during An Evening of Wonders, a large metal box hung from the ceiling throughout. An identical looking box was also used in a performance by Criss Angel on his television series. Both effects involved a prediction that was apparently placed in the box before the show began, and revealed afterwards. A magic fan who has seen both shows might notice that the box appears the same in both programmes and conclude that it must be a trick box. In Underground, Derren did the same trick, but this time used an envelope that was brought onto the stage at the beginning of the second half. By using an ordinary envelope there is no way that the audience could recognise this as a magician's prop that they have seen before, and this gives credibility to the routine. The effect is the same, but there's one less shiny silver box being used, and in a world where magicians seem to use shiny magical boxes all the time this takes the audience's focus even further away from the fact that they're watching a mere trick.

The routines featured in Secret are listed earlier in the book as they were presented in their previous shows. The McFly setup and payoff from the finale of Enigma is presented as the finale to this show, with the objects from Enigma (Egg, Needle, Ice Cream, Goose, Moose, Apple Juice) replaced by animals that are drawn by the audience volunteers. These animals are a Snake, Elephant, Camel, Kangaroo, Sheep and Tiger. In a brilliant addition, the audience members are instructed to draw their animal, and a little extra information must be secretly printed on the cards for some of the volunteers to follow. "Draw Camille, the Camel" could be printed on the card, for example, so that when Derren asks the volunteer what they have drawn he can also prompt "does it have a name?" and the volunteer will say "Camille". This appears to be a free choice of name, but as with so many of the topics we have discussed, nothing is random! During the reveal of the images, we learn that the Camel is called Camille, the Kangaroo is called Roo, and the sheep is actually a female sheep – a Ewe. As with the ending to Enigma, where the initials of the objects on the cards (E for Egg, N for Needle, I for Ice Cream, and so on) spelled out the name of the show, these animals now spell out Secret, once again leading to a standing ovation from the audience.

The audience reaction to every Derren Brown show I've seen has been electric, but for Secret it was an incredible standing ovation. I assume that this show will be televised at some point, but my recommendation is to go and see this show live if you still can – it's a performer at the top of his game and not to be missed.

In this book, we have discussed my theories on all the live shows that you can watch on DVD. My hope throughout is that the reader will learn about magic and showmanship. Perhaps Underground is the test of whether I have put this point across well enough in my writing. If you've read every page of this book and watched all the DVDs you now face a choice. Do you go and see the Underground show, knowing my theories on how the routines are done?

If you feel that there is no need to go and see Underground because you know how it's done then I have not done my job properly. I hope that anyone reading this book is inspired to go and see the show if they have not done so already. Not only is it the best show yet, but I am hopeful that you will take away so much more from the experience by understanding the incredible amount of work that has gone into the production.

We live in an age where you can use Google to find the answer to almost any question. There are those that believe that magic is simply a puzzle to be solved, and those that believe that a knowledge of magic secrets destroys any enjoyment you could take from the show. This is an argument that has raged for years among the magical fraternity. "Keep the secrets secret". I disagree. Growing up, I found that magic was a difficult hobby to get into if there were no magic clubs in your area. I'd ask the questions, but no-one would tell me. I longed for a book like this, that would give me an understanding of magical thinking and theory.

Today, it's all out there on the internet. Whether you watch videos on YouTube, Google for information or read publicly visible pages on magic forums, you can usually find the information you are looking for. But does knowing the secrets make you a magician? Most importantly, does knowing some secrets ruin the magic?

My view is that a show of the complexity of Derren Brown's work is improved when you have some knowledge of what the methods might be. It is true that some magic can be spoiled by knowing the secret, but this tends apply to magic that wasn't particularly strong in the first place. With the kind of magic you witness in any of Derren Brown's work a little knowledge goes a long way to increasing your enjoyment of the presentation as a whole. When you're watching a Derren Brown show, live in the theatre, it's as good as it gets. I hope you see this show yourself, and I'm sure you'll agree.

Afterword: The Masked Magician.

When I was a kid, there was a TV show called, "Magician's Secrets Revealed". This started as a one-off TV Special that purported to reveal magicians closely guarded secrets. The show was very popular and spawned a series, with many tricks being revealed in every episode. Initially, magicians were furious about this because they don't want people to know how the tricks are done. People proclaimed that the Masked Magician was destroying the art of magic by explaining the methods. Looking back on this period, the show actually seemed to have done some good. It didn't kill off the art of magic, but I know of many people who found this show fascinating and developed an interest in magic themselves. Knowing some of the secrets is a great way to get involved, and maybe one day become a performer yourself – I know I did. I really enjoyed the Masked Magician programmes, but there was one thing that used to really annoy me about them, and I'll try to put that into words here.

The shows narrator often had a sneering approach to the performance. When the trick was revealed, he'd often say something like, *"and now you know the secret. Huh.*

Not very magical, is it?" This is not the approach I think the show should have taken. With hindsight, the Masked Magician tended to reveal big stage illusions. You know the sort of thing; you've probably seen a lot of them if you watched TV in the 1980s or have ever been on a cruise ship. The magician wheels out a big cabinet onto the stage, the assistant climbs into the cabinet, they are bound and shackled. The cabinet is covered with a curtain, or perhaps swords are sliced through it. Or maybe the assistant turns into a tiger? We've seen it all before.

The masked magician showed us that the girl slid into a secret compartment, or pulled a hidden lever. Magic allows us to suspend our disbelief whilst we watched the performance, but if we did choose to ponder on how it worked, did we really think she disappeared by magic? Or did we assume a lever was hidden somewhere? The masked magician didn't give away secrets in that sense, he merely confirmed your suspicions if you wondered how it was done.

There's a very famous routine called Metamorphosis, which the Masked Magician revealed on one of his shows. The magician is locked in a trunk, and his assistant stands on the top of it. A curtain is raised, and then dropped to reveal that the magician is now standing on the trunk. He unlocks the trunk to find his assistant inside.

Metamorphosis became the signature routine for Jonathan and Charlotte Pendragon, who performed this on television many times. Their version of Metamorphosis was flawlessly choreographed every time, and the moment where the assistant and magician change places was done in the blink of an eye. It's a good trick but when the Pendragons do it, it's absolutely extraordinary.

When the Masked Magician performed the trick, the method he used was probably similar to that of the Pendragons, but Instead of the split second changeover that they perfected, the Masked Magician laboured over the switch, lifting the curtain multiple times. Eventually, the Metamorphosis happened, and the magician had changed places with the assistant. The trick was explained in detail, and the sneering narrator told us how it's not very magical now you know the methods.

Some would accept that and believe they now know the answer. Not me. The narrator continued to explain magical methods throughout many episodes and often threw in a smart-alec line about how it's not magic at all. But I've seen the Pendragons perform their Metamorphosis many times. It really is magical. It's one of the greatest pieces of magic I have ever seen. For the Masked Magician to reveal the secret wasn't an issue for me, I wanted to know. But, the TV show presented magic as merely a puzzle to be solved. There was no discussion of the artistry, the performance, the skills of everyone involved to make such a wonderful piece of entertainment. They seemed to believe that once you knew the secret that was the end of it. Even now, twenty years on, no-one's done Metamorphosis with the speed and artistry of The Pendragons and it remains a classic of magic. As with all magic, it's not what you're doing, it's how you present it.

For me, knowing the secret is the start of your journey into magic. Now you have read the methods that I believe Derren Brown and his team use, I hope this insight has allowed you to see the sheer glory of the presentation of the theatre shows. As I mentioned at the beginning of this book, knowing Derren Brown's methods is like knowing how Beethoven plays the piano. Sure, he's simply pressing the notes at the right time and in the right order, but can anyone simply take that information and play the piano as well as Beethoven did? Of course not. But what if Beethoven's piano playing inspired you to not only learn to play, but to innovate, to compose, to push boundaries and come up with things no-one has ever done before? That's what I hope is the purpose of this book.

We live in an age where you can find many tricks exposed on the internet. It can be easy to find explanations of where the hidden lever may be hidden, or how the magician lifts two playing cards whilst pretending to lift only one. But it's the practice, the artistry and the performance that separates the tedious pub performer, the bore at the bar and the tacky cruise ship act from the world class performances you see in a live Derren Brown show. If you take one thing away from this book, it should be that the best magic doesn't need complex methods and trickery. It needs real magic, showmanship, flair and charisma. Now you know these methods, I hope that you can see clearly that maybe 10% of what you see is the mechanism behind the performance; the other 90% is the performance itself. If you read this book in order to find answers to your puzzles then that's up to you. I hope that as you finish reading, you have a better understanding of the importance of performance. If you're a magician, I hope this helps as you apply what you have learned to your own show. Make your "Perfect Five Minutes" more perfect. Consider what you do from the audience point of view. Have you created a simple puzzle to be solved, or something that will live with the spectator as a show they will never forget?

You can do better – we all can. As we live in a world where the answer to any question can be found in seconds on the internet, it's time to make magic awesome again. Understand the ideas, learn as much as you can from others, but then use that knowledge to come up with your own magic. When you think you've created something good, think about what else you can do to make your magic bigger and better. As Derren and his team show, the hard work will make it all worth it, and who knows, maybe one day it will be you on the stage receiving that standing ovation.

Printed in Great Britain
by Amazon

69218067R00099